Kenn Bennett's

SECRETS TO ENJOYING
YOSEMITE VALLEY

CONTENTS

Introduction   1
- My Perfect Two Days ...   2
- The Three Parts of Yosemite   6
- When to Go   7
- Top 10 Valley Secrets   9
- Getting There   11
- Admission   12
- Taking the Bus   13

What to See   14
- Waterfalls   15
- Rock Formations   19
- Meadows and Rivers   20
- Manmade Sights   22

What to Do – Activities   25
- Art Classes   26
- Biking   26
- Climbing Programs   27
- 50/50 Valley Driving Tour   27
- Fishing   32
- Hiking   32
- Horseback and Mule Rides   33
- Moonlight Walks   33
- Photography   34
- Rafting   36
- Ranger Programs   36
- Rock Watching   37
- Star Gazing   38
- Swimming   38
- Theater   39
- Tours   39
- Winter Activities   41

Hikes and Walks	43
• Essentials for Hiking	44
• Tunnel View Climb	46
• Bridalveil Fall Walk	47
• Boot Lot Walk	49
• Housekeeping Camp Bridge Walk	52
• Four Waterfalls Hike	54
• Mirror Lake Semi-Loop	60
• Backside of Mirror Lake Hike	62
• Ahwahnee to Mirror Lake Loop	62
• Yosemite Village Meander	66
• Lower Yosemite Fall Walk	70
I Don't Recommend …	73
The Park Beyond the Valley	76
What to do with Kids	81
Where to Sleep	85
Where to Eat	96
Shopping	107
Other Things…	112
• Valley Services	112
• Shuttle System	115
• Wildlife	119
• Bear Rules	121
• Plants	121
• Geology	122
• Historical Timeline	124
• Links and Maps	125
• About the Author	126
• Photo Information	127
Did You Enjoy?	129
Coming Soon	130

INTRODUCTION

The Yosemite Valley is one of the most beautiful places in the United States and the world. The waterfalls, sheer cliffs, granite domes, meadows and wildlife make it, in the words of John Muir "... *by far the grandest of all the special temples of Nature I was ever permitted to enter."* The Valley allows you to see spectacular sights and also lets you escape from daily pressures. A short walk takes you away from most people and opens incredible vistas.

I've written this guidebook to help what I call an "average person" get the most out of a visit to Yosemite Valley. It is not a guidebook that will teach you how to climb El Capitan or backpack for a week in the High Sierra. Those are topics that are covered far better in other publications. My standard for writing this guide is; what is the best advice I can give to my family and friends, so they can enjoy their limited time in Yosemite.

I express opinions in my guidebooks. This is not simply a listing of what exists in Yosemite Valley. I've been many times over many years and learned to like certain places and experiences. I've also learned what, in my opinion, you should avoid. Hopefully you will agree with my thoughts. If not, please don't take it personally if I felt your favorite place isn't worth a visit.

So this is how I recommend you visit the Valley in a short period of time…

MY PERFECT TWO DAYS AND ONE NIGHT IN YOSEMITE VALLEY

I live in Southern California, a six hour drive from the Valley, so I won't go unless I can spend at least two full days there. For me, this itinerary is best when I can go mid-week in the early summer – say the first week of June. Then all the waterfalls are still flowing and the roads to the Mariposa Grove and Glacier Point are usually clear of snow and open. I cheat and actually leave home after work the evening before and drive about 4 hours to Oakhurst and spend the night in a motel. That way I can really get two full days in the Valley.

The next morning, I get up, pack my daypack and have breakfast so I can leave early enough to drive the 20 miles which take 30 minutes, and still arrive at the Mariposa Grove parking lot by 8:30 am. I'm covering a lot of ground today, so to avoid hiking up an 800 feet elevation gain, I will take the first Big Trees Tram Tour in the morning up to the museum in the

Upper Grove. I get off the tram at the museum and will be able to walk among the giant sequoia trees by myself after the tram leaves. I walk the two miles downhill, back to the parking lot, passing through the California Tunnel Tree and by the Grizzly Giant on the way.

Now I drive 37 miles, taking about 75 minutes to reach the Valley. After I go through the Wawona Tunnel, I park in the parking lot on the right side and do the Tunnel View Climb. After enjoying the view without crowds or buses, I start my 50/50 Valley Driving Tour. First stop is the Bridalveil Walk and then I stop at Swinging Bridge Picnic Area to take the Boot Lot Walk (my favorite Valley jaunt). I add the Lower Yosemite Fall Walk and marvel at the view where John Muir chose to build a cabin. Then I complete the loop of the Boot Lot Walk through Cooks Meadow, over Superintendent's Bridge and by Sentinel Meadow till I return to Swinging Bridge.

Now I drive my car to the Day Use Visitor Parking Lot and catch the Valley Shuttle Bus at Stop 1. I go to the Ahwahnee Hotel at Shuttle Stop 3. I walk into the hotel and then into and through the Ahwahnee Bar and find a seat outside, where I will have a late lunch with a view of Glacier Point. When I'm satisfied with food and beverage I'll walk back into the Ahwahnee and maybe just sit for a moment in the Great Lounge and peak at the scrumptious Dining Room.

Then I walk back through the hotel lobby and through the right side parking lot so I can take the Ahwahnee Hotel to Mirror Lake Loop Hike. I pass over the runoff from Royal Arch Cascade and arrive at Mirror Lake late in the afternoon and will have missed the earlier crowds. I'll sit and look at my favorite view for a while and then hike to the back side of the Ahwahnee Hotel. I walk across the back lawn and marvel at a three way view of Yosemite Falls, Half Dome and Glacier Point.

I catch the Shuttle again and get off at Shuttle Stop 4, to avoid a big loop to the Yosemite Lodge, and walk back to my car. Then I drive to Curry Village and check into my tent cabin. I move my food from my car to the bear box outside my tent cabin and then walk over to the Pizza Deck for dinner with a view and meet some new friends from all around the world. About 30 minutes before sunset I grab my folding chair from my car and walk over to Stoneman Meadow. I sit my chair down on the boardwalk and wait with a book and a beverage until the sun starts setting and then enjoy the alpenglow on Half Dome. I stay and watch the stars come out. After the show I walk back to Curry Village, take a shower and set my cell phone alarm for an early wake up for day two.

The morning of day two I take the instant oatmeal, fruit and tea I brought with me, over to the Dining Pavilion and heat water in a microwave available there and make my tea and oatmeal for my quick and cheap breakfast. Then I pack my car and daypack, check-out and walk to Happy Isles and start my Four Waterfalls Hike. I hike past Vernal Fall all the way up to Clark Point. I return via the John Muir Trail. After the round-trip hike, taking four hours and about 4.5 miles, I'm back at my car, still parked at Curry Village.

I hop in my car and drive the remainder of the 50/50 Valley Driving Tour, stopping to admire the view at Valley View. Then I drive the 30 miles that take about an hour, up to Glacier Point. I'll briefly stop at Washburn Point and gaze at the Giant Staircase I was climbing a few hours ago and then continue onto Glacier Point. If I'm hungry I'll stop at the snack bar there and grab some food and take it out to the amphitheater to eat with Half Dome as my companion. Finally I'll walk to Glacier Point and look down over 3,000 feet into the Valley where I hiked, ate and slept yesterday. When I've had my fill of the view I head out for the six hour trip home.

Here's the itinerary summary:

- Mariposa Grove
- Tunnel View Climb
- 1st Half of 50/50 Valley Driving Tour
- Bridalveil Fall Walk
- Boot Lot Walk
- Lower Yosemite Fall Walk
- Lunch at Ahwahnee Hotel Bar
- Visit Ahwahnee Great Lounge and Dining Room
- Ahwahnee to Mirror Lake Loop Hike
- Dinner at Curry Village Pizza Deck
- Alpenglow and star watching in Stoneman Meadow
- Sleep in Curry Village tent cabin
- Self-catered breakfast
- Four Waterfalls Hike
- Snacks on the trail
- 2nd Half of 50/50 Valley Driving Tour
- Valley View Stop
- Washburn Point Stop
- Glacier Point and lunch

Whew, I'm tired just listing it all! I've just covered every major sight in Yosemite Valley in less than 48 hours. I really prefer a more leisurely visit that allows more contemplation of the scenery and life but this is how to cram it all into a short time span.

Now I wasn't always so organized in my Valley visits. I don't even remember what I saw on my first trip when I was in college. I just know I couldn't pronounce Yosemite (I thought it was yose-might instead of yo-sem-it-e). On my second visit, car trouble caused my friends and me to arrive at Tunnel View at 3 am, so tired that we just rolled out our sleeping bags and slept there in the parking lot until dawn (definitely not recommended and illegal).

THE THREE PARTS OF YOSEMITE, OR WHY THIS BOOK ONLY COVERS THE VALLEY

Most people hear the name Yosemite and think immediately of the Valley. (Not to be confused with the Southern California valley used by "Valley Girls" or the Central California agricultural giant called the San Joaquin Valley). The Yosemite Valley includes the glacier carved valley with big, vertical cliffs, the well-known waterfalls and much of the park's visitor services. These sights are the really unique parts of the park and the reason most visitors come to Yosemite National Park and why this book only covers the Valley. My website offers hikes and suggestions on where to go and what to do in the rest of the park.

The Valley is only a small portion of the park. North of the Valley are two small groves of giant sequoia trees, another glacier carved valley called Hetch Hetchy that is drowned beneath a reservoir for San Francisco drinking water, and the high country of forests, lakes and granite along the Tioga Road (Highway 120) and Tuolumne Meadows. This high area along Tioga Road is normally only open from late May, when the road is first cleared of snow, until snow closes the road again, usually sometime in November.

South of the Valley are the spectacular views from Glacier Point and the Badger Pass Ski Area. Further from the Valley are the Wawona area and the Pioneer Yosemite History Center. Close to the South Entrance is the Mariposa Grove of Giant Sequoias. The roads to Glacier Point and the Mariposa Grove can be closed in the winter as they are not cleared of snow.

WHEN TO GO

Most people visit the Valley in the summer and this leads to large crowds and parking issues. In fact two-thirds of the 3.9 million visitors come in the summer when many Valley waterfalls are dry. You should avoid the Valley this time of year if you can. If summer is your only choice, try going during the week and definitely avoid Memorial Day, 4th of July and Labor Day. People from surrounding areas know there are far fewer people in autumn, winter and early spring.

If you are a waterfall fanatic, then late April, May and early June is the time for you. The crowds are not quite as large and all the waterfalls are flowing normally. The higher elevation roads may still be closed due to snow, but the Valley and usually Mariposa Grove are accessible.

Late autumn, winter and early spring are the times I have en-joyed Yosemite Valley the most. Fewer people means the park is easier for you to enjoy with less frustration over parking, lines or noise. The same rocks, trees and views are there year round. The trails in the Valley are open unless you happen to see snow, which can occur a few times a year. I especially like winter to avoid crowds. Note that weekends and holidays still may have crowds. The only potential issues with winter are possible road closures due to snow, any snowy weather lead-ing to requirements to use chains on your tires, and possible Mariposa Grove and especially Glacier Point road closures. But you can ice skate at Curry Village and ski at California's first ski area, Badger Pass. See the box for year round tem-perature and precipitation information.

Average Temperatures and Precipitation for Yosemite Valley											
	Jan	Feb	Mar	Apr	May	Jun	Jul	Aug	Sep	Oct	Nov	Dec
Temperature ° F												
Max	49	55	59	65	73	82	90	90	87	74	58	48
Min	26	28	31	35	42	48	54	53	47	39	31	26
Precipitation												
Inches	6.2	6.1	5.2	3.0	1.3	0.7	0.4	0.3	0.9	2.1	5.5	5.6

TOP 10 VALLEY SECRETS

1. Stay in the Valley. You'll save yourself hours of driving on mountain roads.

2. Book lodging as far in advance as you possibly can. You'll have more options and be more likely to stay where you want. The Delaware North Company (DNC), manager of all Valley lodging options, takes reservations starting 366 days in advance. You can usually cancel Valley lodging reservations without a penalty if you cancel at least 7 days in advance.

3. Stay in Curry Village. Yes it's probably going to be a tent that costs as much as a chain motel room outside the park and you will hear the voices of hundreds of people, but this is the last Valley lodging option to fill up and you can frequently find last minute reservations here. And hey you will be in a beautiful National Park so why not try camping the easy way?

4. Be early. There are only so many hotel rooms and campgrounds in the Valley. Everyone else drives or takes a bus to the Valley. So if you get up early and beat those commuting people, your preferred sight or activity will be much less crowded than after about 9 am.

5. Stay late. All those people who drive to the Valley in the morning will drive out of the Valley late in the afternoon. Sights are frequently empty after 5 pm.

6. The best photography times are early or late in the day.

7. Have lunch at the Ahwahnee Hotel. While others are fighting crowds at Valley sights, you can relax and enjoy one of the most beautiful dining rooms in the USA with fewer people and at a lower cost than dinner.

8. Get away from the roads and Shuttle Buses. The further you walk away from Valley roads the fewer people you will see. My favorite getaway hike? My Four Waterfalls Hike to Clark Point above Vernal Fall. Bonus Secret: Wear the right footgear for a more pleasant hiking experience.

9. Bring at least some of your own food, beverages and snacks. Food is expensive and time consuming in the Valley. Plan to feed yourself for at least one meal a day.

10. Bears will make your car into a picnic basket. It's a federal fine if you leave food in your car overnight. Use your hotel room or bear locker at your campground to store your food and avoid the fines and repair bills if a bear chooses to open your picnic basket (I mean your car!).

Bonus Secret: Getting Around the Valley on a Very Busy Summer Day.

Don't drive, don't even take the Shuttle. Traffic may be so slow that your fastest way to get anywhere in the east part of the Valley is to walk or bike. If you don't have your own bike, be sure to rent early to avoid a sell-out.

Bonus Secret: Outside the Valley Hint

Drive up to Glacier Point if the road is open (usually May to November). This is one of the best viewpoints you will ever see. It's well worth going out of your way and making the time to do this. Added Bonus: Go in the evening on a clear night for a fantastic star show after you take in the view.

GETTING TO THE VALLEY

Getting to the Yosemite Valley means you need to have motor vehicle transportation. You can't fly; take a train or a boat to the Valley. You can use public transportation to get to the Valley but you have to work at it and a bus is your only public option to actually reach the Valley itself. The simplest way is to drive, and since almost everyone does, a lot of traffic and parking hassles can result. Depending on where you start from, you can enter the Valley via four entrances. Typically people coming from Southern California enter at the South Entrance via Fresno and Oakhurst on Highway 41. From the Bay Area and Northern California people can choose from the Arch Rock Entrance through Merced via Highway 140, or the Big Oak Flat Entrance from Groveland via Highway 120. Visitors from the Eastern Sierra, Reno and Mammoth use the Tioga Pass Entrance, from Lee Vining via Highway 120. These four roads into the park all merge at various points until they are all funneled onto the one-way Southside Drive just north of the parking lot for Bridalveil Fall. My website has a chart that shows driving times and mileage from all over California.

All of these routes require some driving on mountain roads with speed limits of 35 miles per hour so it takes quite a while to actually reach the Valley even after you have entered Yosemite National Park. Note that the Tioga Pass Entrance is normally only open from about June to October due to snow. At times in the winter you may have to use the Arch Rock Entrance since it is the lowest elevation entrance and usually receives the least snow. Also know that you must carry chains when driving in the winter as they can be required at any time because of ice or snow.

The fastest time from park entrance to the Valley Visitor Center is from the Arch Rock Entrance Station and that is still 20 minutes of driving time assuming perfect road and traffic conditions. It takes 45 minutes from the Big Oak Entrance, 1 hour from the South Entrance and 1 hour, 45 minutes from the Tioga Pass Entrance. When you double these times for a round-trip I think you will understand why I strongly recommend you stay in the Valley instead of driving in from outside the park each day you visit! There are usually lines at the entrances if you come during a peak travel time. I've had to wait as long as an hour just to get into the park on a summer Saturday around 10am because of the crush of people all trying to enter at the same time.

ADMISSION FEES

Yosemite National Park charges an entrance fee of $20 per vehicle. If you walk in or ride a bike, motorcycle or horse the fee is $10 per person. The fee is good for 7 days of unlimited entrances. Be sure to save your receipt as you may be checked when you depart or need it to get in without paying a fee later in the week.

There are several passes you may want to purchase if you are a frequent visitor to Yosemite or other national parks. You can buy an annual Yosemite Pass for $40 at any park entrance. Obviously if you make more than two visits a year to Yosemite you will save yourself money by buying this pass. I personally buy the America the Beautiful–National Parks and Federal Recreational Lands Annual Pass for $80 a year because it saves me time and money when I visit all the parks I frequent each year. You can also get this at an entrance or buy it in advance. See my website for details and the link. Finally there are two lifetime admissions and discount passes for US citizens or permanent residents; the Senior Pass costs $10 for those age 62 and over and the Access Pass is free for those with permanent disabilities. Both can be obtained at a park entrance or in advance by providing appropriate documentation and an additional $10 fee.

TAKING THE BUS

If can't drive you will need to take a YARTS (Yosemite Area Regional Transportation System, 1-877-989-2787) bus into the Valley. You will have to get yourself to Merced in order to catch a YARTS bus. You can do that via Amtrak trains, Greyhound buses or Great Lakes Airlines flights from Los Angeles and Las Vegas. Making a connection may require you to stay overnight in Merced. There currently are no bus routes from Fresno or Groveland to Yosemite. YARTS does run a route from Mammoth and Lee Vining over Tioga Pass to the Valley in the summer months. See my website for appropriate links.

WHAT TO SEE – VALLEY SIGHTS

These are the reason you come to the Yosemite Valley. Most of the sights listed here are outdoors and available year round. I've included my own rating system for these sights.

Kenn Bennett's Rating System	
✸ ✸	Shouldn't Miss
✸	Should Make an Effort to See
	Worth Knowing About
🚶	Included in a hike later in the book

The sights are organized by type below. The section on the Shuttle System has a summary of what's where by Shuttle Stop.

WATERFALLS

The waterfalls of Yosemite Valley are legendary and include two of the ten tallest waterfalls in the world. However if you come to the Valley in late summer you may only see one waterfall actually with water. That is Bridalveil Fall which normally flows year round. The other falls visible from the Valley are ephemeral, meaning they dry up after all the snow in their watershed melts. If you love waterfalls, the moral of this section is visit the Valley April – June when the most water is flowing down the waterfalls.

I've listed the Valley waterfalls below in the order you see them as you drive into the Valley on Southside Drive and then out of the Valley on Northside Drive.

Silver Strand Falls – This waterfall is seldom seen by visitors since there are no signs pointing to it or trails leading to it. The best place to find this 1,170 feet tall waterfall is from Tunnel View. To find this waterfall from the parking lot closest to the Valley, look toward Bridalveil Fall and then follow the south rim of the Valley to your right till you are almost looking above the Wawona tunnel. Way up there on the south rim is Silver Strand Fall. Sometimes in the winter you will see a frozen waterfall instead of a flowing one.

❋ ❋ 🕈 **Bridalveil Fall** – This is the one waterfall that you can almost always count on to actually be flowing because the watershed that feeds it is fairly large and has a lot of soil that holds water better than just rocks. Wind can blow the water stream sideways when there is less water running down the 620 feet drop, thus creating the veil effect for which the waterfall is named. You should hike the trail that ends close to the base of the waterfall. To help you gauge the height of

Bridalveil Fall, think of Seattle's Space Needle which is 605 feet tall.

※Ribbon Fall – Best seen from Southside Drive just past the junction of Southside Drive and Highway 41 to Wawona and Fresno, Ribbon Fall at 1,612 feet tall, is the Valley's tallest free-leaping waterfall. This is an ephemeral fall that usually dries up by late summer. This waterfall is to the left of El Capitan on the north rim of the Valley.

Sentinel Falls – This 2,000 feet tall fall is the 7th tallest in the world. You can see it from the trailhead for Four Mile Trail and from Swinging Bridge. It flows from spring to late summer in a series of drops or cascades from the south rim of the Valley to the west of Sentinel Rock.

Staircase Falls – Found above Curry Village, this waterfall flows 1,300 feet in stair step fashion from Glacier Point to the Valley.

Illilouette Fall – This is one of the least seen of all the falls in the Valley. You can only see it if you hike on the John Muir Trail toward Vernal Fall. This 370 feet tall fall provides more water to the Merced River than any other Yosemite waterfall. This is one of the four waterfalls you can see on my Four Waterfall Hike. Best seen from what I call "photo rock" on that hike. You can also see just the top of it from Washburn Point on the drive to Glacier Point.

※🚶 Vernal Fall – The bottom step of the Giant Staircase, Vernal Fall is 317 feet tall. A good comparison is the Statue of Liberty which is 306 feet tall. You must hike to see this one too but it is well worth the effort. It is also visible from Washburn Point. The Mist Trail gets its name from the mist thrown onto the trail by this waterfall.

❋🏃 **Nevada Fall** – The top step of the Giant Staircase, Nevada Fall is 594 feet tall. The Washington Monument is only 555 feet tall. You can't see this waterfall until you hike to the top of Vernal Fall; so many people only see it from the distance of Washburn Point. Both Vernal and Nevada Falls typically flow year round, though with much decreased volume after the spring to early summer snow melt.

Almost all the previous Falls were on the south side of the Valley and now the list swings to the north wall.

🏃 **Royal Arch Cascade** – This 1,250 feet tall cascade is best viewed from the back lawn of the Ahwahnee Hotel. You can walk to the creek flowing out of the base of the cascade on my Ahwahnee Hotel to Mirror Lake Loop Hike. This cascade is visible just to the left of the Royal Arches rock formation after a heavy rainfall.

Lehamite Falls – Another ephemeral waterfall, is located above Yosemite Village. This one has not even had its height measured because you only see it in the spring and after big rainfalls. Cooks Meadow is the best place to view this waterfall but most people miss it since they tend to focus on the next listing from there.

❋❋🏃 **Yosemite Falls** – This is the biggy around here and at 2,565 feet tall is the 5th tallest waterfall in the world and the tallest in North America. Visible from many places in the Valley, I prefer the view from either Cooks Meadow or Swinging Bridge. Unfortunately this one can dry up so to avoid disappointment don't expect to see it in late summer or early fall. When flowing at full strength you can hear these falls all over the Valley if you stop and listen for it. Yosemite Falls has three parts, the Upper Fall is 1,430 feet tall, the hard to see middle cascade is 675 feet tall and the Lower Fall is 320 feet tall. Be sure to take the walk to the base of the Lower Fall. This is one of the most popular sights of the Valley so try visiting early in the morning or late in the afternoon to avoid the crowds.

Horsetail Falls – This is the fall famous for turning red or orange in late February with the right weather conditions. I tried to see it in 2011 but gave up because it was so crowded with photographers. Know that you need a fairly good camera and long lens to really capture the effect in a photo. This fall is 1,000 feet tall and only flows in the late winter to spring when the snowfall accumulated on the top of El Capitan melts. It is best seen from El Capitan Picnic Area on Northside Drive or .8 miles east of Cathedral Picnic Area on Southside Drive.

The Cascades – Technically this isn't in the Valley but just west of the Valley on Highway 140. There is a parking lot at the base of this 500 feet tall waterfall on the road to the Arch Rock Entrance.

So that's the list of the 13 named waterfalls flowing into the Valley. If you are lucky enough to be in the valley after a rain storm you may find water flowing down the valley walls almost everywhere. By the way, did you notice sometimes I called these water features fall and other times falls. It's technically a fall if the water flows straight from the top to bottom without getting diverted on the way. Think Bridalveil Fall. If the water hits rocks and changes course it's called falls like Yosemite Falls.

Waterfall Height Summary (with comparisons)	
Name	Height in Feet
Yosemite Falls	2,425
Sentinel Falls	2,000
Willis (Sears) Tower – Chicago	*1,729*
Ribbon Fall	1,612
Empire State Building – New York	*1,453*

Staircase Falls	1,300
Royal Arch Cascade	1,250
Horsetail Falls	1,000
Eiffel Tower – Paris	*986*
Lehamite Falls	Uncertain
Gateway Arch – St Louis	*630*
Bridalveil Fall	620
Nevada Fall	594
Washington Monument	*555*
Illilouette Fall	370
Vernal Fall	317

ROCK FORMATIONS

The Valley is ringed by walls of granite that rise up to over 4,000 feet above the Valley below. Many of these walls have named rock formations. Below is a short list of ones you won't want to miss.

✳**El Capitan** – This is the largest granite monolith in the world. It towers 3,614 feet above the floor of the Valley below. You see this rock from Tunnel View and can also see it very well from El Capitan Meadow. I like to bring my folding chair and binoculars and find a climber or two and watch their progress for a few hours. The ascent can take days but someone once did it in just under 3 hours. For comparison the Rock of Gibraltar is 1,398 feet tall or less than half as high as El Capitan.

✳ ✳ **Half Dome** – This rock formation is visible from just about anywhere in the east end of the Valley but there are especially good views from Sentinel Bridge and Cooks Meadow. This granite dome looms 4,748 feet above Mirror Lake below. Half Dome competes with Yosemite Falls for the prize of the most photographed feature of Yosemite. Some people ask where is the other half. The answer is there probably wasn't another half; it was never a complete dome.

✴**Glacier Point** – This point rises 3,242 feet above Curry Village below. It is easily seen from Curry Village, Stoneman Meadow and the Ahwahnee Hotel. While impressive from below its even better when you are on top looking down into the Valley.

MEADOWS AND RIVERS

The reason I visit the meadows of the Valley is because they offer the best views of the rest of the Valley. They are also a great place to see wildlife, especially at dusk or dawn. Please respect these meadows by staying on the trails and boardwalks. Just imagine how hard it would be for you to grow if nearly 4 million people walked on you every year. These meadows are listed below from west to east as you drive in on Southside Drive and then out on Northside Drive.

🚶 **Sentinel Meadow** – This meadow is just after Swinging Bridge Picnic Area. Almost everyone stops here for the views of Yosemite Falls. The Yosemite Chapel is at the east end of this meadow. My Boot Lot Walk goes along this meadow.

Stoneman Meadow – This meadow is across from Curry Village and has nice views of Half Dome, Glacier Point and Yosemite Falls.

✳🚶 **Mirror Lake (Meadow)** – This is a lake that is quickly filling and becoming a meadow. You have to hike or bike here and this is the featured destination for three of my hikes. The famous reflections of Half Dome in the waters of Mirror Lake are still there in the spring when Tenaya Creek is running high, but may disappoint you later in the summer or autumn. Still, this is a nice place to get away from the rest of the Valley even though this is one of the most popular hiking destinations.

Ahwahnee Meadow – A meadow to the east of Yosemite Village and across from Church Bowl Picnic Area on the road to the Ahwahnee Hotel. A webcam shows the view of Half Dome from here.

✳✳🚶 **Cooks Meadow** – This is my favorite meadow of the Valley. It is across Northside Drive from Shuttle Stop 6 for Yosemite Falls. The view here features Half Dome or Yosemite Falls. You can get here from either Shuttle Stop 6 or 11. I like to bring my folding chair in the evening and just sit listening to Yosemite Falls, watching alpenglow on Half Dome and watching the stars come out. I almost always see deer somewhere in this meadow and have also seen coyotes here. I am constantly amazed at how little foot traffic this meadow has given its location with world class views and both Northside and Southside drives only a few hundred feet away. This meadow is featured in my Boot Lot Walk.

El Capitan Meadow – This meadow is located just after the Northside junction with the cross over road back to Southside Drive. It offers the best place to see El Capitan and thus the rock climbers. Please stay on the paths here to avoid trampling the delicate plant life. This is another location I like to bring a chair and just sit. This meadow is really quiet during early morning hours.

Merced River – This River runs the entire length of Yosemite Valley from Vernal Fall until it exits at the west end. You are never far from the Merced and there are many locations to enjoy the scenery as the River flows by. My favorites include the bridges in the Manmade Sights, Cathedral Picnic Area and the Happy Isles area.

MANMADE SIGHTS

Nature is the real hero of Yosemite Valley; but there are a few buildings, bridges and museums you should know about.

✳🚶 **Valley Visitor Center** – The Visitor Center for Yosemite Valley is a little different than those in most other National Parks in that you cannot just park in front and walk in. You should park at the Day Visitor Parking Lot and then either walk about ½ mile or take the Shuttle Bus to Stop 2 and walk the rest of the way. Once inside the entrance there is a large relief map of the Valley that I find enlightening in understanding the geography of the Valley. Behind this map is a desk manned by Rangers who will answer all your questions. To the left is the Bookstore run by the Yosemite Conservancy and to the right is a series of small exhibits on the geology, plants, wildlife and human history of Yosemite. You should not miss the "Spirit of Yosemite" film shown every 30 minutes in the theater behind the Visitor Center.

🚶 **Yosemite Museum and Indian Village of Ahwahnee** – Located next to the Visitor Center and built in 1925, this is the first museum built by the National Park Service. Today it houses rotating exhibits on the history of Yosemite and a collection of Indian craft works. Frequently you find demonstrations of various crafts such as jewelry or basket making. Behind the Museum is a self-guiding tour of what an Ahwahneechee community may have been like in the 1870s.

🚶 **Happy Isles Nature Center** – This is located at Shuttle Stop 16 and offers natural history exhibits and children's nature programs. Open May to September.

🚶 **Yosemite Chapel** – This is the oldest structure in Yosemite, holding religious services since 1879. Now a nondenominational chapel, various services are held throughout the week. My oldest daughter swears she will be married here though at this writing I'm unaware of any candidates to help her with that. Parking is next to the Chapel, but you must come to this from the west on Southside drive. You can also take a short walk from Shuttle Stop 11 to reach the Chapel. The Chapel is also featured in my Boot Lot Walk.

❋ ❋ 🚶 **Ahwahnee Hotel** – This hotel has a marvelous Grand Lounge featuring huge fireplaces, stained glass windows and paintings and artifacts from Yosemite's history. Anyone can visit this lounge and adjoining rooms and you definitely should, even if you are not staying or dining here. This is the one manmade place in the Valley you should not miss. The easiest way here is to take the Shuttle to Shuttle Stop 3, although there is a small but usually full parking lot.

The following is a list of bridges I believe you will find useful. They are listed from west to east.

🚶 **Swinging Bridge** – This footbridge is located at Swinging Bridge Picnic Area just east of the Yosemite Chapel. I feature it in my Boot Lot Walk. This bridge has one of the best views of Upper Yosemite Fall.

❋ 🚶 **Superintendent's Bridge** – You won't find this footbridge named on most maps of the Valley. It crosses the Merced

River, south of Cooks Meadow and offers a convenient way to walk from Yosemite Falls to the Yosemite Chapel. You will frequently have this bridge to yourself. This bridge is also used in my Boot Lot Walk.

Sentinel Bridge – This bridge is famous for its view of the Merced River with Half Dome rising above. This is a two way auto bridge that gets crowded with people and cars daily and is also full of photographers fighting for a good angle to shot Half Dome looming above. I personally feel that Cooks Meadow or the Merced River behind the Day Visitor Parking Lot offers better shots of Half Dome.

✳🚶 **Housekeeping Camp Bridge** – I have asked Rangers what this bridge is named and no one and no map has given me an answer, so I am just calling it Housekeeping Camp Bridge (like my creative name?). This footbridge crosses the Merced River behind Housekeeping Camp and goes to what was one of the Riverside Campgrounds before the flood of 1997 washed that campground away. The bridge is still here and offers views of Glacier Point and Yosemite Falls. I like to stand here anytime Housekeeping Camp is closed and just watch the clear water flow by. In the summer months this bridge can be loud and crowded by the residents of Housekeeping Camp. You can reach this bridge by taking the Shuttle to Shuttle Stop 12, crossing the road and following the river to the bridge. This bridge is featured on my Housekeeping Bridge Walk.

🚶 **Ahwahnee Bridge** – Years ago, this was an auto bridge but is now a bike and foot bridge behind the Ahwahnee Hotel. Reach it by going through the Ahwahnee Hotel lobby and walking across the back lawn until you reach the Merced River and the Ahwahnee Bridge. The bridge has nice views of the hotel, Glacier Point and when flowing, Royal Arch Cascade. This bridge is on my Ahwahnee Hotel to Mirror Lake Loop Hike.

WHAT TO DO - ACTIVITIES

There are lots of things you can do in Yosemite Valley, including many you can't do anywhere else. This section has the overview of these options and some, like hiking, have greater details in following sections. Up to date availability and rates for all activities are found at the Yosemite Variables page on my website. And be sure to check out the Yosemite Conservancy Events Calendar (link at my website) and the current Yosemite Guide Events and Programs schedule. I always look at last year's Yosemite Guides (links on my web site) to get ideas on what happened last year during the season I am planning to visit this year. Finally check the deals section of my website for updates on coupons and promotions for Valley activities. The "Passport" you get for supporting the Yosemite Conservancy changes yearly and has had coupons for things like 2-for-1 bike rentals or horseback rides in the past.

ART CLASSES

The Yosemite Conservancy sponsors art classes from April to October at the Yosemite Art & Education Center in Yosemite Village. These classes are held Tuesday through Saturday from 10 am to 2 pm. A $5 donation is requested for each student. Students under 12 years old must be accompanied by an adult. You must supply your own materials or purchase them at the Center. All classes are outside, weather permitting. You should sign-up in advance by calling (209) 372-1442. You will be asked to pay a $5 pre-registration fee, which will be applied to the donation request when you attend the class. A link to the schedule of classes is available at my website.

BIKING

Biking is allowed in the Valley on all paved roads and on over 12 miles of designated bike paths. Because of car traffic, riding your bike may actually be the fastest way around the east end of the Valley in the summer and on busy weekends and holidays. All children under age 18 are required by California law to wear a helmet while biking. There are no mountain bike trails in Yosemite and bikes are not allowed off paved roads or trails anywhere. No motorized bikes or scooters are allowed. The most popular bike path is the one to Mirror Lake, but you must park your bike before you reach the Lake and walk about a quarter mile to reach it. Go early to avoid the crowds. If you don't have a bike or don't want to haul it to the Valley, rentals are available spring to fall at Yosemite Lodge and Curry Village. Rental is by the hour or day. See current hours and rates at my variables web page. Rent early during the summer to avoid sell-outs. The rental includes a bike helmet. I recommend you take a ribbon or

scarf to tie onto your bike when you park it so you can identify it among the masses of rental bikes. Also know you must
follow the traffic rules if you ride on any of the Valley roads.
This has caused some cyclists grief when they go the wrong
way on either of the one-way Northside or Southside Drives.
For example, if you go past Camp 4 on Northside Drive, you
can't legally get back to Yosemite Village without going for
an almost 6 mile loop all the way to El Capitan Meadow and
back on Southside Drive.

CLIMBING PROGRAMS

The Yosemite Mountaineering School and Guide Service has
been teaching rock climbing in the Valley since 1969. This is the
only rock guiding service allowed in the Valley. Their classes
are offered daily at 8:30 am from April to October and typically
last about 7 hours. They offer classes for all experience levels
from beginning to expert and also have classes specially geared
for women. Classes start at their office in Curry Village. They
strongly encourage advance reservations which can be made
by calling (209) 372-8344 or emailing them at yms@dncinc.
com. I have to admit I'm more than a little nervous around
heights so I haven't tried any of these classes, but several Boy
Scout leaders I trust highly recommend the programs here.

DRIVING TOUR (AKA 50/50 VALLEY DRIVING TOUR)

Most people drive to Yosemite but I can't really recommend you do a lot of driving around the Valley. It's just too

congested and hard to park to justify using your car as a means of getting from point A to point B in the east end of the Valley, where many of the sights, activities, lodging and foodservice are located. But in the west end of the Valley you can only get around by driving, biking or walking. And if you drove to the Valley you have to go through this west end to get to most of the things you will want to do. So this is my suggested driving tour. I call this the 50/50 Valley Driving Tour because you should do half on your way into the Valley and the other half on the way out of the Valley. I assume you will be driving in and out of the Valley during daylight hours. This tour isn't much fun in the dark!

There are three routes into the Valley. Highway 41 from Fresno and the South Entrance, Highway 140 from Merced to El Portal and the Arch Rock Entrance and Highway 120 from Modesto or Manteca to the Big Oak Flat Entrance. This last route gets to the Valley via the Big Oak Flat Road that merges with Highway 140 at the west end of the Valley. Highway 120 is also the route from Tuolumne Meadows and Mammoth. All of these routes come together at a point close to Bridalveil Fall and become Southside Drive.

Stop 1. If you are coming from the south on Highway 41 you will go through the Wawona Tunnel right before you enter the Valley. When the tunnel ends you are presented with one of the most fantastic views in the world. This is known as Tunnel View. El Capitan is on your left, Bridalveil Fall on your right, the Valley in the center and Half Dome in the distance. You may have seen a very famous Ansel Adams photo of this view. You will want to park and get out of your car and take in this view and take the traditional photos here. There are parking lots on the left and right as you exit the tunnel. I prefer the one on the right because no buses park in it, I find it easier not trying to turn left across the uphill traffic and it tends to be less crowded. Be sure to use the crosswalks and use care if you choose to cross the highway to get to the viewpoint on the other side of the road. This is also where the hike

I call Tunnel View Climb starts. I think this is one of the little known secrets of the Valley and offers similar views without so many people.

Stop 2. From Tunnel View, continue downhill for about 1.5 miles and you will find the entrance on the right to a parking lot for Bridalveil Fall. I suggest you go into the lot and quickly cruise the loop to see if you are lucky enough to find a spot. Don't worry if you don't and definitely don't waste time driving the loop hoping for someone to leave. Simply go back to the highway, turn right and then almost immediately right again. Within a few hundred yards you will find adequate parking on both sides of the one-way Southside Drive. This location also has good views of El Capitan and Ribbon Fall. My walk on Bridalveil Fall has the details of walking close to the base of the waterfall.

I haven't left those of you arriving in the Valley on Highways 120 or 140 off the tour. About a half mile after these highways merge, you will reach a junction where you must turn right and go over the Merced River on the Pohono Bridge. You are now on a one-way road and will follow this almost 1 mile until you reach signs that point right for Highway 41 to Wawona and Fresno. You turn right at this intersection and continue past Bridalveil Fall and about 1.5 miles uphill until you are at Tunnel View. This is stop 1 above. When I want to stop at Tunnel View on my way out of the Valley I will use the parking lot on my right side and then walk across the road to take the Tunnel View Climb route. After you are finished at Tunnel View you retrace your route downhill and stop at Bridalveil Fall, Stop 2 above.

Stop 3. From Bridalveil Fall you will continue to your next stop at Cathedral Beach Picnic Area. If you parked in the Bridalveil parking lot you exit by turning right. You turn right again onto the one-way Southside Drive. Be sure to take the time to see El Capitan and Ribbon Fall on the left. Now you continue for just over 1.5 miles. You cross another junction on the left that would allow you to exit the Valley but continue straight ahead on Southside Drive for .1 mile. The entrance to Cathedral Beach Picnic Area is on the left. There is parking on the left just beyond the entrance if you are here when the picnic area is closed. I actually prefer this spot in the late fall to early spring timeframe, when the picnic area is closed, because the short walk in discourages many people from visiting the area. You either drive or walk to the picnic tables and restrooms close to the Merced River. Walk from the parking area to the gravel beach along the river. El Capitan is to your left. Look between the trees behind you and you can see both Cathedral Rocks and Cathedral Spires. The Spires are the twin shafts that loom 1,936 and 2,147 feet above the Valley floor.

Stop 4. Continue east on Southside Drive (the only way you can drive since this is a one-way road) for almost another 2 miles and you will come to Swinging Bridge Picnic area. There is parking on the left here that fills quickly or you can continue past and shortly find parking along Sentinel Meadow. This is the start of what I call "Boot Lot Walk" which is my favorite in the Valley, but you can simply walk to the bridge over the Merced River. This bridge was once a suspended bridge and thus called Swinging Bridge. The name has stuck long after that old bridge was replaced. The view upriver is one of the best in the Valley of Upper Yosemite Fall.

This is the end of the driving tour into the Valley. After Swinging Bridge you will see the Yosemite Chapel on the right and then a junction where you continue straight to Curry Village or turn left over Sentinel Bridge and onto the Ahwahnee, Yosemite Village or Yosemite Lodge. All of these locations are accessible via the Valley Shuttle and thus not included on this driving tour.

When you leave the Valley, be sure to allow some time for a few stops on your way out. This driving tour starts on Northside Drive, just after the Yosemite Lodge.

Stop 5. From Yosemite Lodge you drive about 2.5 miles to El Capitan Meadow. This meadow is just after a junction on the left that would allow you to circle back to the east end of the Valley. There is parking on both sides of the road here, but I prefer the left side since this allows a better view of El Capitan. I find binoculars useful here to find climbers on the face of El Capitan. This is the closet you can drive to this huge chunk of granite. If you turn and face the opposite direction you have a view of Cathedral rocks.

Stop 6. Continue 1 mile on Northside Drive from El Capitan Meadow and you will reach a nice view of Bridalveil Fall. There is parking on the left side of the road that is right next to the Merced River.

Stop 7. About .8 miles from the Bridalveil Fall view you come to Valley View. This viewpoint is also on the left and comes up fairly quickly so be sure to get in the left lane at about a half mile from the previous stop. Remember this is still a one-way road. Valley View is another quite famous location for photographs and from the parking lot right next to the Merced River the view features El Capitan on the left, Bridalveil Fall, Cathedral Rocks and Leaning Tower on the right and the Valley and Merced River in the center of the view. Most people have no idea there is a restroom across the road from this view point. Be careful crossing the road if you choose to use these facilities.

That's the last stop on my driving tour. In about another ¼ mile you come to an intersection where you turn left for Highway 41 to Fresno or to return to the Valley. You continue straight for Highways 120 and 140.

FISHING

You can fish in the river and streams of Yosemite Valley from the last Saturday in April to November 15. If over 16, you must have and clearly display a valid California Fishing license. Licenses and gear can be purchased at the Yosemite Village Sport Shop. Rainbow trout are catch and release. Catching brown trout has a 5 per day limit or 10 in possession. Only artificial lures or flies with barbless hooks are allowed. No live bait is allowed. The Merced River is open to rafts, kayaks or canoes from the Stoneman Bridge at Curry Village to Sentinel Beach Picnic Area so you will want to avoid this section. Also no fishing is allowed from any of the bridges. I won't pretend I know much about fishing so suggest you ask at the Sport Shop or Visitor's Center if you want tips on good fishing holes.

HIKING

This is my favorite activity in the Valley as you can probably tell from the number of hikes in this book. Let me say here that I am thoroughly convinced the best way to enjoy the Valley is to get out of your car or off the Shuttle Bus and walk. The farther away you walk from roads the fewer people you will see. And the better prepared you are for a hike the more you will enjoy it. Specific details on individual hikes are in the Hikes and Walks section. And be sure to read my "Essentials for Hiking" list.

HORSEBACK AND MULE RIDES

The only stables in the valley are located next to North Pines Campground at Shuttle Stop 18. They offer mainly mule rides from April to October. You must be over 7 years old and 44" tall and weigh less than 225 pounds to ride. They offer rides to Mirror Lake that follow the trail I describe in the "Backside of Mirror Lake" hike and takes about 2 hours, and a half day ride up to Clark Point via a stock only trail as far as the Vernal Falls footbridge and then the John Muir Trail, for views of Vernal and Nevada Falls. As with most activities here, reservations are strongly recommended and are available by calling (209) 372-8348.

MOONLIGHT WALKS

If you are in the Valley on a clear night, with a three-quarters to full moon, be sure to get out to a meadow after dark. Turn off all light sources and look to the north Valley walls. I am always amazed at the amount of moonlight that can be reflected off these walls. I find this simple experience to be one of the most awe inspiring sights of Yosemite. My favorite meadows for these "Moon Walks" are Cooks and Stoneman Meadows, which just happen to be a short walk from respectively the Yosemite Lodge or Curry Village. The back lawn of the Ahwahnee serves the same purpose. I just stand or sit on my trusty folding chair, look at the walls and moon and listen for waterfalls and animals. It's handy to have a flashlight or headlamp to get to the meadow, but be sure to turn them off once you have arrived. My website has a link to a website that will calculate moon phases and moon rise and set times for Yosemite Valley Visitor Center for any month you select.

PHOTOGRAPHY

Anyone who comes to the Yosemite Valley should plan on taking just a few pictures. Sure you've probably seen pictures of the Valley but there is nothing that adds more to your memories of your visit than your own photos. Ever since I bought a digital camera, I take tons of photos to help me remember what I've seen and what I want to write about. Below is a listing of locations you might want to consider for photo opportunities.

The stops from the 50/50 Valley Driving Tour above offer great photo locations. Those are:

- Tunnel View

- Bridalveil Fall

- Cathedral Beach

- Swinging Bridge Picnic Area

- El Capitan Meadow

- Bridalveil Fall View

- Valley View

Other locations mentioned in my hikes section include:

- Superintendent's Bridge (Boot Lot Walk)

- Sentinel Bridge (Boot Lot Walk)

- Muir Cabin Location (Lower Yosemite Fall Walk)

- Yosemite Falls (Lower Yosemite Fall Walk)

- Mirror Lake Stairs (Mirror Lake Hike)

- Vernal Fall (Four Waterfalls Hike)

- Clark's Point (Four Waterfalls Hike)

- Housekeeping Camp Bridge (Housekeeping Camp Bridge Walk)

- Merced River behind Day Visitor Parking Lot (Housekeeping Camp Bridge Walk)

I don't pretend that I'm a great photographer. I only use a small "point and shoot" digital camera but believe I occasionally manage to get some decent photos. You can see color copies of the photos in this book and many other ones at the Yosemite Photos page of my website. I've also listed what I feel is the best photo guidebook to Yosemite on that webpage. That guidebook not only discusses where to take photos in Yosemite, but also the time of year and time of day to get the best shots.

RAFTING

This is definitely a summer activity and the Park Service only allows rafting under the perfect conditions, but boy is this fun! This isn't white water rafting, but just a lazy way to pass an afternoon on the water. You can raft on the Merced River when the flow is not too high or too low. Typically this occurs in June and July but varies from year to year. The water temperature plus the air temperature must equal 100° F or greater for the river to be open and you can only raft from 10 am to 6 pm. The allowed stretch of the river is from Stoneman Bridge near Curry Village, 3 miles downriver to Sentinel Beach Picnic Area. Going this entire stretch will take you 3 to 4 hours depending on how energetic (or lazy) you are in paddling and stopping along the way. Only non-motorized craft like rafts, canoes and kayaks are allowed and you must have personal floatation devices immediately available for everyone in your boat.

All this leads me to recommend that you rent a raft rather than bring your own. The folks at the Curry Village Recreation Center will know if the river is open and have everything you need for rafting. The rental price includes a free ride back to Curry Village at the end of your trip. The rafts hold four adults. Children are less expensive on the rental rate chart but must weigh 50 pounds to take the ride. I recommend you pack a lunch and beverages in a cooler and take your time down the river.

RANGER AND DNC PROGRAMS

The NPS and DNC offer a wide range of events and programs to help you learn about and enjoy the Valley. Every day you will find a wide variety of options available to entertain you and your family for free. DNC also has some walks or programs available for a fee but I admit I have never paid for one since there are so many free options. I always go online and print out the current Yosemite Guide before I leave for the Valley so I can decide what programs I want to do during my trip. My favorite programs include traditional campfire programs, twilight or moonlight walks and ranger strolls on various topics.

ROCK WATCHING

This may sound a little weird, but trust me; rock watching is a great activity to do in Yosemite Valley. First remember that this Valley is very unique and that when you are in the Valley you are surrounded by granite walls that tower thousands of feet above you on at least two sides and maybe more when you are in the east part of the Valley. Then also realize that these walls offer little to help you realize the scale of their size. My favorite way to explain this is to talk about Yosemite Falls which tumble 2,425 feet from top of the wall to the Valley floor below. Now can you tell me how high that really is? Well here's a way to think about it. The Empire State Building in New York City is "only" 1,453 feet tall to the top of its lightning rod. You still need almost another 1,000 feet tall to reach the top of the Valley wall at Yosemite Falls. Try stacking the Eiffel Tower (986 feet tall) on top of The Empire State Building and you would still be 76 feet from the top. See what I mean about no way to understand the scale of these very tall granite rocks. So to try and grasp the immensity of the walls around me, I like to just sit in a meadow and look at the rock walls; thus rock watching. I pull out my folding chair and sit. Sometimes with a snack or beverage or a book but mainly just watching the rocks go by. This "activity" is best with few people around so I prefer either early morning or late afternoon.

Late afternoon on a clear day may offer the bonus of seeing alpenglow on high up rocks like Half Dome which can glow orange, red and purple from the indirect light of the sun that has just set. Try watching the wind move jet contrails above the walls. Good places for rock watching are any areas with a view unobstructed by trees. I like to sit in Cooks Meadow or along the Merced River at Cathedral Beach Picnic Area.

STAR GAZING

You can see stars on any night that is clear and moonless. For us city dwellers it is an eye opening experience to see how many stars are really out there when you remove city lights. Just like the moon walks above, all you need is a clear night, a meadow and a flashlight and you can see stars! Again I like Cooks and Stoneman Meadows for this activity. (Behind the Ahwahnee doesn't work as well since it's easier to see stars without any light pollution). Just get to an open space, turn off your lights and look up. I always take a star chart so I can identify the star formations and constellations.

SWIMMING

Swimming on a hot summer day is any kid's dream. In the Valley they can do that at Curry Village or the Yosemite Lodge even if you aren't staying there. There is also a year round pool, for guests only, at the Ahwahnee Hotel. You can also swim in the Merced River but need to use good judgment when doing so. There are no lifeguards on the river. Do you know where all the water in the river comes from? Try melting snow. That means even in the summer the water is COLD so even good swimmers can easily get hypothermia and be unable to swim. So be careful if swimming in the river.

THEATER

The Yosemite Conservancy sponsors programs in the Yosemite Theater behind the Valley Visitor center. This is the same theater you can watch the "Spirit of Yosemite" film during the day. These programs are typically run in the late spring to early fall 5 or 6 days a week. In the past the programs have included Tom Bopp with a live musical and multimedia performance highlighting Yosemite's history and Lee Stetson as John Muir among the animals or telling stories of John Muir's life. These are usually fun shows and tickets are available at the door, at the Conservancy Bookstore at the Visitor Center or at any DNC Tour and Activity Desk.

TOURS

DNC offers a variety of tours in or from the Valley. These are especially useful if you lack your own car. If you have a car you may prefer to transport yourself so you can save money and follow your own schedule. All these tours start at Yosemite Lodge. Reservations can be made in the Valley at any Tour & Activity Desk located at Yosemite Lodge, Curry Village and the Village Store or at the concierge at the Ahwahnee Hotel. These tours can sell out so if you are sure you want to take one you can also call (209) 372-4386 in advance to reserve before you arrive.

The first and most popular option is the Valley Floor Tour. This is a two-hour tour that is available year round. This tour makes a big loop of the west and east ends of the Valley. The route follows exactly my 50/50 Valley Driving Tour above and adds on Shuttle Stops 12 through 21 so you really can see all these sites without paying for this tour. A park ranger narrates the tour and does provide some interesting insight about what you will see. The tour makes two stops, first at Valley View and then at Tunnel View. These stops are the only reason I can recommend this tour. If you don't have a car, getting to these locations requires you to walk a good distance farther than most of us would want to walk. I especially believe everyone should see Tunnel View so take the tour if you can't drive there. In the warmer months you take the tour sitting in an open air tram that is essentially a flat-bed semi-truck with seats. It looks a little strange but is an enjoyable ride. In the colder months this tour is given in a normal tour bus.

The next tour isn't really in the Valley but features Glacier Point which offers a great view of the Valley. The Glacier Point Tour is only available when the road to Glacier Point is open, which is usually May to October. This four hour tour also stops at Tunnel View since you must go on Highway 41 through the Wawona Tunnel to reach Glacier Point. You can buy a one-way ticket if you want to walk down to the Valley from Glacier Point via the Panorama Trail (a long and strenuous but beautiful hike).

The last tour I will mention is called the Grand Tour. This all day tour starts at 8:45 am and includes the Glacier Point Tour above and goes onto Wawona and the Mariposa Groove of Sequoia Trees. Time for lunch is allowed at Wawona but is not included in the tour price so you may want to pack your own. There's not much that I find particularly interesting in Wawona but you should make an effort to see giant sequoia trees. This tour is best for someone without a car or for someone who just doesn't like to drive. If you drove to the Valley via Fresno on Highway 41 you really don't need to take this tour since you pass everything going to the Valley and again on your way out.

WINTER ACTIVITIES

The Valley is open year round and much less crowded in the winter. Many activities are limited by the weather (who wants to go rafting when you have to chip ice off your paddles!) but there are a few things only available when the temperature drops. The first of these is the outdoor ice skating rink at Curry Village. This location features a very nice view of Half Dome and an outdoor fire perfect for marshmallow roasting. Bring your own s'mores supplies and save on the high prices in the rental store. Beside skate rentals and smore supplies, the rink side rental store also has the always appreciated hot drinks. The ice rink is normally open November to March.

Yosemite also features the oldest downhill skiing area in California. While not in the Valley, Badger Pass Ski Area is a basic ski location on the road to Glacier Point that features mainly beginner to moderate ski runs. DNC operates a free bus service twice a day each way for those staying in the Valley at a DNC property. In addition to downhill skiing, the area also offers snowboarding, cross-country skiing, snow shoeing, equipment rentals, lessons and snow tubing. While this is a fun for the whole family place, I feel it's really out of place in a national park. I don't come to Yosemite to ski but many people disagree with my feelings. If skiing is your thing you can have fun here.

The other winter activity I frequently partake of in Yosemite Valley is fireplace watching. Most of the lodging options have fireplaces somewhere in them and I make full use of them in the winter. My favorites are the ones in the Ahwahnee Great

Room. Even if you aren't staying at the Ahwahnee you can sit by the fire and just enjoy the atmosphere for a while. Also nice are the fireplaces at the entrance to the Curry Village Dining Pavilion and in the Mountain Room Lounge at the Yosemite Lodge.

HIKES AND WALKS

This section describes hikes that start in the Valley. These are the very best ways to enjoy the Valley as well as get away from the crowds that tend to congregate close to the roads. Generally the longer and farther the hike takes you from a road, the fewer people you will share the trail with. My favorites on this list are Boot Lot Walk and Four Waterfalls Hike. These hikes are listed from west to east in the Valley along the south side of the Valley and then back out of the Valley from east to West on the north side.

Please be sure you are prepared to take these hikes. I am frequently amazed to see hikers walking in sandals or barefoot and carrying no water or map. My list below summarizes what you really should have with you on any Valley hike away from civilization.

ESSENTIALS FOR HIKING

• Appropriate footwear – at a minimum you should have sturdy, broken in, tennis shoes. Sandals or less really aren't going to offer support to your ankles or insteps. Light weight hiking boots are better. Heavy boots are really more than you need for any of the hikes in this section

• Socks – along with the boots you should have appropriate hiking socks.

• Daypack – or least some way the carry the rest of the list with you on your hike. And no a grocery store bag is not going to cut it here. You need something to get things out of your hands and on your back or in pockets.

• Water – You need to drink while you are walking. Many of these hikes do not have drinking fountains available and you never should drink from a river or stream without purifying the water first. Even water bottles from a store will suffice.

• Food – at a minimum you should bring a few snacks for everyone on the trail with you. Maybe you need to bring breakfast and/or lunch as well. I prefer snacks that are easy to eat while I'm walking like granola bars, gorp or fruit.

• Trash bag – somewhere to put the trash you will generate on the trail. You will pick up after yourself, right? If you bring a big one it can also double as a rain coat if you are caught in a storm or are hiking close to roaring waterfalls.

- Sunglasses, sunscreen and sun hat – you don't want to get sunburned do you? My balding top never forgives me if I forget my hat!

- Camera – your cell phone may suffice here (but don't plan on cell service), just be sure you have some way to record the memories you make on the trail. Bring a plastic bag to protect it if you will be close to any raging waterfalls.

- Flashlight/headlamp – just in case you lose track of time and need to hike home in the dark.

- Map – you should always have a map that covers where you plan to walk. Get a hard copy and don't count on your cell phone or GPS unit. All the hikes in this section are covered on the NPS "Yosemite Valley Hiking Map" available online so you can print it before you come (see the maps section) or pick one up for free at the Valley Visitor Center before you head out.

- Binoculars – this is really optional but I know I enjoy having my small pair along to increase my viewing options.

- Common Sense – allow yourself enough time to enjoy the hike and really look around and experience your surroundings. Be sure to stay on the trail so you don't get lost and don't damage plants or contribute to erosion. Bring your car keys and identification! Just in case.

The hikes and walks:

TUNNEL VIEW CLIMB

This is a very short hike I use to better enjoy Tunnel View. Many people have no idea this trail exists and just a few hundred yard walk yields a better view, fewer people and no bus fumes.

When to go: Every day. The trail may be icy in the winter but is usually passable for the short distance I recommend you walk it.

Length: A few hundred yards. This trail climbs 500 feet in elevation in just over half a mile but I only go as far as it takes me to feel like I have escaped the hordes below me. If you were to continue up another 500 feet and half mile you would reach Inspiration Point where Ansel Adams took his famous shot of a thunderstorm over Yosemite Valley. Allow 15 minutes unless you just want to drink in the view longer.

Directions to the start: This trail starts at the Tunnel View parking lot on the south side of Highway 41. This lot is the one on the side of the road away from the Valley, not the more crowded one that more directly overlooks the Valley. You must drive here as there is no trail to Tunnel View. There are stairs up the side of the Valley, close to the trashcans. This is the start of the climb.

Facilities: None

The Climb

I call this a climb because the trail starts as stairs and continues up for 1000 feet in about a mile. I never go higher than a few switchbacks. This is just enough to get away from all the people who stop to see the breathtaking view from the parking lot known as Tunnel View. It's just a simple short walk up until I decide the view is good enough and I can no longer smell the fumes from the cars and buses. The view is a great reason to linger and I have frequently brought a lunch with me and found a rock to sit on and simply watch the clouds go by.

BRIDALVEIL FALL WALK

Bridalveil Fall is the first waterfall you see when entering the Yosemite Valley. It's a 620 feet tall waterfall that doesn't look that big. Imagine the Seattle Space Needle there and that's how tall it is. You can fight for parking and take a half mile round-trip walk to the closer up view.

When to go: Bridalveil is one of the few waterfalls in the Valley that flows year round. It is most spectacular in the spring and early summer. Go early in the morning if you want to avoid parking hassles and crowds.

Length: ½ mile round-trip if walking from the Bridalveil Fall parking lot. If parked on Southside Drive the walk is .8 miles round-trip. Allow one hour. The walk gains 50 feet in elevation.

Directions to the trailhead: The only way to see the base of Bridalveil Fall is to drive or walk there. The parking lot is on Highway 41. If you are headed into the valley you will pass (and probably stop at) Tunnel View. Continue downhill from Tunnel View about 1.5 miles and the parking lot will be on the right side, just before you merge with Southside Drive. The parking lot holds about 50 cars and will be crowded unless you get there early or off season. If cruising a parking lot while hoping someone leaves to give you a spot is not your idea of fun, continue right on Highway 41 to Southside Drive. You can only turn right as this is now a one-way road into the Valley. Shortly after you turn there is parking on both sides of the road. Park on the right side for safety and find the .4 mile trail back to the waterfall. If you are driving from the east end of the Valley you need to follow Northside Drive until you reach the Pohono Bridge. Follow signs to Wawona, Highway 41. You cross the bridge, driving one-way back toward the Valley. At the intersection with Highway 41 you will need to turn right and the fall parking lot will be almost immediately on your left.

Facilities: There are a set of 6 (smelly) pit toilets in the southwest corner of the parking lot. No other facilities.

The Walk

From anywhere on the south side of the parking lot you can see the entire length of the fall through the trees. This is the last place you can see the entire fall. You will find the trailhead at the east end of the lot. You follow a wide paved, trail to a fork in the trail just before a bridge. Follow the sign to the right, along the south side of a stream. This trail is one of my favorite places in Yosemite to listen to the visitors talk. See how many different languages you hear. Continue up the path. Be prepared to get wet in the spring. The winds that helped Yosemite Indians give the fall the name Pohono may be evident. Pohono is thought to mean evil or puffing wind. The same wind can push the stream of the fall outward until the falling water looks like a "bridal veil". There is usually a crowd at the viewpoint. A favorite photo opp of my family is to look at the boulders behind the viewpoint in the fall and early winter. Fallen leaves gather here and make a great spot for kids to play. Also be sure in the spring and early summer to look behind you, across the valley. There almost directly behind you is a view of Ribbon Fall. It is normally dry by early summer.

If you are parked on Southside drive you follow a former road bed toward the fall. You will also have great views of Ribbon Fall and El Capitan if you look the opposite direction. You will cross three bridges over Bridalveil Creek and then turn left onto the path uphill to the overlook.

Return the way you came, being sure to watch for traffic in the parking areas.

BOOT LOT WALK (AKA VALLEY LOOP)

Boot Lot is the Bennett family name for the Valley version of Swinging Bridge. (There is another bridge named Swinging Bridge over the South Fork of the Merced River near Wawona). This is a level walk along the Valley bike path so you can also bring or rent a bike and wander along this wonderful path. When my children were small we brought along those folding scooters and let them ride along that way. Sure cut down on the "I'm tired" whines! This is our favorite walk in Yosemite!

When to go: Year-round.

Length: 2.3 miles loop. Allow 2 -3 hours. Level all the way. You can easily add a jaunt to the base of Yosemite Falls, a side trip for a gorgeous view of Half Dome from Sentinel Bridge, or a wander around Yosemite Village to this walk.

Directions to trailhead: Since this is a loop you can start just about anywhere. This narrative starts at Swinging Bridge and goes clockwise, but it is also easy to start at a number of other spots including Yosemite Lodge at the Falls (stop 8 on the Shuttle), Lower Yosemite Fall (stop 6) and Sentinel Bridge (stop 11). You can also park along Southside drive between Swinging Bridge Picnic Area and the Yosemite Chapel. You'll know you are in the right area by the view of Yosemite Falls.

Facilities: Restrooms are available at the Swinging Bridge Picnic Area, Yosemite Lodge at the Falls, and the entrance to the path to the base of Lower Yosemite Fall. Water is available at the hotel and the start of the Yosemite Falls path. Food can be purchased at the hotel. Bike rentals are available in season at the hotel.

Why do I call this Boot Lot Walk? My family went to Yosemite between Thanksgiving and Christmas for years until the kids were heading to college. One mid-December we had the little ones in snow boots and parked at the Swinging Bridge lot and took this walk. The next day one daughter was missing a snow boot. We went back to the parking lot and there in the middle was the missing boot. My daughter took her boots off before getting in the van but somehow one of them failed to make the final few inches inside. And the park was so empty that the boot was still there 24 hours later. Thus we call this "Boot Lot" and the walk from it bears the name in that boot's honor.

The Walk

We start this walk from Swinging Bridge. There are pit toilets here and a picnic area. The bridge over the Merced here has a view of Upper Yosemite Fall that is my favorite in the valley. When my children were young we would play "Poohsticks" for hours from this bridge (found in the Disney Winnie the Pooh "A Day for Eeyore" video.) After the bridge, the path follows along the river on the right and Leidig Meadow on the left. Follow the path to the right when a Y intersection offers a path to Camp 4.

Be aware of bikes on the path if you are walking. The path soon goes through some housing units for DNC staff and then between the river and buildings of the Yosemite Lodge at the Falls. We frequently see deer here along the riverfront. The path continues through the hotel grounds until you reach Northside Drive. Be careful crossing here. You will then be at the start of the walk to the base of Lower Yosemite Fall. See my Lower Yosemite Fall Walk for more details. This is a side trip we always take and well worth the time. Be sure to look down the path for a great view of Lower Yosemite Fall if you choose to pass on this side trip. If you are biking you will have to park and lock your bike at the start of the walk up to the Fall. There is a real restroom here and water fountains.

The path continues past the restroom, over Yosemite Creek until you reach Shuttle Stop 6. We usually cross back over Northside Drive here but you can continue ½ mile along Northside drive to Yosemite Village from here. See my Yosemite Village Meander for more details on this option. After crossing the road you will be in Cooks Meadow. This is another area where you frequently see deer in the early morning or evening. The path will have another Y junction shortly. The left path heads through the meadow to Sentinel Bridge and a famous view of Half Dome. We take the right fork back to the Merced River. You have good views of Half Dome along the path. Also be sure to look behind you to see Yosemite Falls from another angle.

Shortly you will reach Superintendent's Bridge. This is another excellent "Poohsticks" opportunity and features more nice views of the Merced River. Continue over the bridge until you reach Southside Drive. Here we cross the road so we can visit the Yosemite Chapel. This is a small interdenominational chapel built in 1879 and is the oldest building in Yosemite that is still occupied. It was moved here from the original location at the base of Four Mile Trail. Many weddings are held here so be sure to enter quietly. My oldest daughter claims her wedding will be here. We are still waiting on that.

From the chapel you will need to cross back over Southside Drive. This meadow was the center of activity in the Yosemite of the late 1800s. This "Old Village" was gradually moved to the present location because of floods and the shade. The Valley walls shaded this village so it was much colder than the present Village which gets sunshine longer into the day. The path now continues along Southside Drive and Sentinel Meadow until you return to Swinging Bridge. There is a boardwalk across Sentinel Meadow on the way back to the bridge. The boardwalk takes you back to the Merced River and has plaques that discuss the regeneration of the meadow. Ahead you find the Swinging Bridge Picnic area and you have completed the loop.

HOUSEKEEPING CAMP BRIDGE WALK

This level walk features an unnamed footbridge over the Merced River between Housekeeping Camp and the former Riverside Campgrounds. You won't find this bridge on the NPS Yosemite Valley Hiking Map so it is frequently an empty route. This is a point to point walk from Shuttle Stop 12 for the LeConte Memorial Lodge/Housekeeping Camp and Stop 1 for the Valley Visitor Parking lot. You can also go the other way from Stop 1 to Stop 12, but I prefer the former. I especially enjoy this walk from October to April when Housekeeping Camp is closed.

When to go: Every day. The trail and bridge can get snow covered in the winter but is passable. When Housekeeping Camp is open you may find people fishing or swimming along the trail but the path is normally fairly secluded.

Length: ½ mile one way. Allow 30 minutes unless you plan to retrace your steps then allow one hour. This trail is level, with little elevation gain or loss.

Directions to the start: This trail starts at Valley Shuttle stop 12.

Facilities: You can use the restrooms in Housekeeping Camp or find restrooms next to the Village Store in Yosemite Village. Food and beverages are available in season at the Housekeeping Camp Grocery Store or in Yosemite Village.

The Walk

From the Shuttle Stop shelter there is a crosswalk over Southside drive toward Housekeeping Camp. After you cross the road veer to your right until you reach the Merced River. Follow the river north, away from the road. You will pass in front of the most desired, riverfront camp units, until you reach a footbridge over the Merced. The views from the bridge are of Upper Yosemite Fall or Glacier Point. In the spring and early summer you also can see Staircase Falls flowing down from Glacier Point. I can stand on this bridge for hours just enjoying the clean, clear water of the river and the views. In the summer you will probably see people rafting down the river.

After you cross the bridge you turn left and follow the trail as it proceeds a short distance away from the river. You are walking through the former Riverside campground, which was closed after the floods of January 1999. Continue on the path until you reach Northside Drive. A trail crosses the drive and follows the edge of Ahwahnee Meadow along a group of houses for employees. One of these houses has beautiful dogwood trees that bloom pink in the spring. I normally do not cross the drive but continue along it until I reach the parking lot and Shuttle Stop 1. A short side trip into the parking lot and left will bring you to the Merced River again and a beautiful view of Half Dome looming above the beaches of Housekeeping Camp across the river. From this point I can easily catch the Shuttle, walk to Yosemite Village, or return the way I came to Shuttle Stop 12.

FOUR WATERFALLS HIKE -VERNAL AND NEVADA FALLS

The hike to view these falls is one of the most popular in Yosemite, if not the country. Even though it can be quite crowded this is the one hike you shouldn't miss in Yosemite. I call it the Four Waterfalls Hike because you can see Yosemite and Illilouette Falls in addition to Vernal and Nevada Falls. The last two falls flow over what is frequently called the Giant Staircase in a stair step fashion. These are very big steps, since Vernal Fall is 317 feet tall and Nevada Fall is 594 feet tall. (For comparison the Washington Monument is 555 Feet). Most people should be able to reach the Vernal Fall footbridge and just a little more hiking will yield even better views of Vernal. Beyond that is a strenuous hike that you should only attempt if you are in decent condition. The Mist Trail to the top of Vernal Fall is appropriately named and if you continue that far you should be ready to get very wet. This is also the trail typically used by those wanting to climb Half Dome in the summer months.

When to go: Every day, although it can be icy in the winter. As with other popular Yosemite locations you will find fewer people if you start early, say before 8 am or late, after 5 pm in the summer. In the winter, the Mist Trail may be closed due to icing. These waterfalls flow year round, although the flow may seem skimpy in the late summer through early spring months. Hey at least these falls will really have water in the summer!

Length: 1.6 miles round-trip if you stop at the Vernal Fall footbridge. Allow 1 to 2 hours. (400 feet elevation gain). 2.2 miles round-trip if you continue to my suggested lunch rock stop. (450 feet gain). Three miles round-trip if going to the top of Vernal Fall via the Mist trail. Allow 2.5 to 3.5 hours (1000 feet gain). I do not recommend you continue on to the top of Nevada fall. I usually continue from Vernal Fall to the bridge above the Silver Apron and then to Clark Point to avoid returning via the stairs by Vernal Fall. This route is more mileage than simply returning the way you came but I feel is easier on the knees and is a 4.5 miles loop. Allow 3.5 to 4.5 hours. (1460 feet elevation gain).

Directions to the start: This trail starts at Shuttle Stop 16. If you don't want to take the shuttle you can walk from Curry Village which adds another 1.6 miles round-trip. After the Shuttle Stop the trailhead starts after you cross the bridge over the Merced River.

Facilities: There are restrooms at the Shuttle Stop, just past the Vernal Fall footbridge (closed in winter) and above Vernal Fall. Water is available at the Shuttle Stop and at the Vernal Fall footbridge (also closed in winter). In the summer there is a snack bar at the Shuttle Stop.

The Hikes

From Shuttle Stop 16 you continue across the bridge over the Merced River. You turn right after the bridge and follow the river to a former USGS (US Geologic Service) stream-gaging station. This station was used from 1915 to 2010 to track the flow of the Merced River. Now the station is the small building across the river. The new station has a webcam pointed at the old location. This webcam updates every 5 minutes and I have occasionally seem groups of people standing on the concrete waving at the building across the river for 5 minutes in hopes their friends will see them on the webcam!

At this point you turn uphill on an asphalt paved trail. There is a sign here that discusses the challenges of climbing Half Dome. Shortly you will reach a sign titled "High Sierra Loop Trail" with destinations and mileages. You are bound for Vernal Fall Bridge .8 miles, Top of Vernal Fall 1.5 miles or Emerald Pool 1.6 miles.

The path climbs between the Merced River and a talus slope made of rock falls from the cliffs above. There are no switch-backs or stairs until after the Vernal Fall Bridge. After a quarter-mile you reach an opening in the trees and a wall lined left turn corner in the trail. If you look back toward the Valley from this corner you can see Upper Yosemite Falls. I call the large rock that will be in front of you "photo rock" since groups frequently stop here for pictures. By turning and facing the cliffs directly opposite the Valley view you can find Illilouette Fall high up in the notch above you. Find the top of the notch and look slightly below it and to the left. You have already found two of the four falls on this hike. Illilouette Fall actually provides the largest flow of water into the Merced River of all the tributaries. It is 370 feet high, though you can only see a portion of it. Around the corner the rock wall continues and the trail starts down for a short time. It quickly continues up on a steeper grade. You can see Illilouette Fall from many vantage points along this part of the trail. The trail continues up until you reach the second of two rock falls. Immediately after you pass the second you begin a short descent to Vernal Fall footbridge.

At the footbridge, look to your left and you will see Vernal Fall up the river, framed by trees. This is the point where many people stop. You absolutely should continue just a bit farther for a much enhanced view of the third waterfall on your hike. Across the bridge is a large drinking fountain that is the nicest I have ever seen in a National Park with two sinks, faucets and drinking fountains surrounded by a beautiful granite top. Just past this is your last flush toilet of the hike. Both the drinking fountain and toilet are closed in the winter.

The trail continues up to the left of the toilets. It is no longer paved and now narrower and rockier. On the left are constant views of the Merced River but no real opportunity to view the fall. After .2 miles you come to a junction with the John Muir Trail that bends uphill to the right. This trail continues over 200 miles to Mt. Whitney but is not our route up. Continue straight on the Mist Trail. The metal sign here says .3 miles to the top of Vernal Fall. In the winter the gate here may be closed due to dangerous ice conditions ahead. If open, you will go only a short distance till there is a short metal post on the right side of the trail. This was a sign post that pointed to the left side of the trail and steps toward the river. If you follow these short steps down from the trail you will find a group of rocks and old signs warning that the rocks are slippery even when dry. Carefully go onto the large, flat rock and look upstream for a stupendous view of Vernal Fall. I call this the "lunch rock" since I have eaten lunch here on many occasions. Many people should enjoy the view here and go back to the Shuttle stop by retracing your steps.

Look to the right of the fall and you can see the beginning of the steps you must climb to reach the top of the fall. There are over 600 steps and you can see how wet they are from the spray of the fall. (I lose track every time I try to count them so just know there are more the 600 of these things!) You can choose to turn back from this point or continue. Even if you don't want to go to the top of the fall you may consider going up the trail to the old dead tree by the steps. That spot provides a very up close look at the fall should you choose to tackle only the beginning of the steps.

When the water is flowing high, you will get wet before you reach the dead tree and understand why this is called the Mist Trail. You won't see many photos of this part of the trail because you could ruin your camera if you try to use it from these wet viewpoints. Be sure you have your camera protected! I put mine inside my daypack, but have seen others use plastic bags.

From the old tree the trail turns right and continues steeply uphill. There are small level spots at several points along the way where you can stop and enjoy the drenching. (Also a great excuse to allow others to pass you while you take a rest!). Higher up you will reach a group of trees and finally get out of the spray. This trail circles for a landing by almost looping behind the falls. The final climb to the top is made of steps carved out of the cliff face. This part is essentially one-way so look before you start up. Fortunately there is a hand rail along this portion of the trail.

Once you reach the top, continue to follow the hand rail, now going down to the front edge of the waterfall. The view here is world class. If there are lots of people you may need to take a turn at the edge but the view makes up for any delay. During the late spring and early summer the fall can be 100 feet wide. You already know its 317 feet down and the view continues all the way back to footbridge you crossed earlier.

You've come this far so I recommend you go on just a little further before you decide on which way to go back. The trail can be tough to spot here so just follow along the river and the green colored small lake called the Emerald Pool for obvious reasons. Shortly there will be a pit toilet on the right. The trail is easier to pick up now but I usually stay along the water. You quickly will see a bridge across the river and a chute of water below it called the Silver Apron. This is another favorite place for Bennett family picnics but beware the local wildlife! The birds and rodents here are very aggressive so you will need to guard your food to avoid feeding the locals.

The trail to the bridge is uphill from the water. Just go uphill and you will find it so you can turn left and continue to the bridge. Just before you reach the Silver Apron Bridge you get a view on the right of the 4th waterfall on this hike, Nevada Fall. You can't really see the fall from the bridge and need to continue on this trail up for a distance to get a better view. This bridge is where I stop. Now you make a decision on which way to go back to the Valley. Retrace your steps and its 1.8 miles, over 600 steps and a 1,165 foot elevation loss back. Instead you could continue up to Clark Point and you will go up another 300 feet over .4 miles of switchbacks. The reward for going higher is constantly improved views of Nevada Fall, a very nice view down to Vernal Fall, no drenching on the Mist Trail and NO STEPS to kill your knees. This route is .9 miles longer than retracing your route but it's the route I prefer.

From Silver Apron Bridge, retrace your steps back along the trail a short distance toward Vernal Fall. You will see a sign on the left that says Nevada Fall 1.6 and Yosemite Valley 2.7. This trail up is what I consider the easy way back. You will climb switchbacks the whole way up but I truly believe this is easier than the 600 step alternative. Each switchback to the left will provide you with a higher and better view of Nevada Fall. After you have climbed for a few minutes you need to watch on your right for a short side trail that will take you to the best view of Vernal Fall. This is easy to miss so be alert. This side trip is worth the view back down to the fall and Emerald Pool.

You continue up to a trail junction at Clark Point. From this point you could continue left 1.2 miles to the top of Nevada Fall or right 5.2 miles up to Glacier Point. I took my wife up the Panorama Trail to Glacier Point many years ago and nearly paid for it with a divorce. So now I recommend following the trail down to Yosemite Valley. This portion of the trail follows switchbacks for 1.3 miles and down 900 feet but really isn't too tough going this way. This is again called the John Muir Trail and meets the Mist Trail at the junction you passed earlier. Turn left at the junction and proceed across the Vernal Fall Footbridge to the Valley.

MIRROR LAKE (MEADOW) SEMI-LOOP

Mirror Lake was formed by a rock fall across Tenaya Creek. Since that occurrence the creek is trying to reclaim the lake bed by filling it yearly with silt. There are still impressive reflections of Half Dome, Ahwiyah Point and Mount Watkins in the spring and early summer. The Park Service dredged the lake for years and used the sand on winter roads. Since that practice has ended, the lake is slowly filling up and will eventually become a meadow. A rockslide in 2009 closed the loop trail so now you can only walk part way around the loop to Snow Creek Bridge. This is now one of three routes to Mirror Lake and is the most commonly used route. I prefer the other two routes since they are less crowded but both are more work than this classic route.

When to go: Every day. The best reflections in the lake are normally early in the morning or late in the afternoon or early evening. The "lake" usually is dry by late summer but there is still a pleasant walk along Tenaya Creek. This walk is especially nice in late spring and when the dogwood trees may be in bloom. This is one of the most popular hikes in Yosemite so I strongly urge you to get here early, preferably before 9 am. You could also go late in the afternoon to avoid crowds, say after 5 pm in the summer.

Length: Two miles round-trip if you stop at the Upper Pool of the lake. Allow 1-2 hours. The walk to Mirror Lake gains 100 feet. Taking the semi-loop to Snow Creek Bridge adds another

2.2 miles. Allow 2-3 hours total time and expect a 200 foot elevation change.

Directions to the start: This trail starts at Valley Shuttle Stop 17. If you don't want to take the Shuttle you can walk from Curry Village which adds another 1.5 miles round-trip.

Facilities: There are two pit restrooms along the trail. The first is much less used than the ones closer to the lake. You will need to bring your own water.

The Hike

From the benches and shelter at Shuttle Stop 17 you follow a paved road all the way to Mirror Lake. The road is only used by bicycles now. There is an unpaved foot trail to the right of the road. This trail rejoins the road at Tenaya Bridge over Tenaya Creek. An alternate trail splits off to the right at this bridge. I describe that in the "Backside of Mirror Lake" hike. A nice view of Half Dome looms above the bridge and creek. The footpath angles off to the left about 200 yards after the bridge. I prefer to stay on the road since it follows the creek and offers much better views and scenery. The only issue with this road is that it is very popular for bicycles. At about ¾ of a mile there is a large bike rack and a sign stating rented bicycles are not permitted on the steep hill ahead. Don't let the sign scare you as the grade is not bad. I believe it might be a little difficult for the bicyclists to control their bike on the way back down so the bike parking area is simply a way to keep the immediate lake area from being overrun with the bikes.

If you go to Mirror Lake in the spring you will find a Lower Pool and an Upper Pool. I have seen people stop at the Lower Pool believing that's all there is to Mirror Lake. Be sure to continue on to the Upper Pool for the best views year round. There are interpretive signs that lead around the edge of lake or meadow. Even in the summer or fall you may find small pools reflecting the images of the granite around you. My secret place to get a shot of the reflection of Mt. Watkins and Ahwiyah Point is opposite an interpretive sign titled "Visitors at Mirror Lake". When you find the sign turn around and find the stairs that appear to lead up to nowhere. I believe these stairs led to the hotel long since removed from Mirror Lake. But they still provide a nice view down onto the reflecting water.

At this point you can return to the Shuttle stop or continue onto Snow Creek Bridge for another 2.2 miles round-trip. This is my preference since crowds thin dramatically after the lake.

The route now becomes a trail and meanders above Tenaya Creek. There is a short upward stretch which provides nice views down to the creek and up to Half Dome. The trail levels and travels through dogwood trees. At the junction to Snow Creek Trail you bear right and continue to two bridges. The first one will probably have you asking why is there a bridge over nothing? The second bridge is a nice foot bridge over Tenaya Creek with views up and down the creek. Since the rock slide there is little incentive to continue from this point. You can take the trail a little over another quarter mile but will find it closed before you approach the actual rock slide. This side of the creek does have the advantage of almost no foot traffic if you want to get away from people. I normally turn around at the bridge and return to the lake and eventually the Shuttle.

BACKSIDE OF MIRROR LAKE HIKE

This is one of three alternative routes to Mirror Lake. This follows the opposite side of Tenaya Creek from the normal route and is inaccessible to bikes so is much less frequented but also does not feature the famous reflections of Half Dome in the water. Instead there are fewer people and reflections of Washington Column.

When to go: Every day. As with the other side of the creek, the best reflections in the lake are normally early in the morning or late in the afternoon or early evening. This hike is on a real trail, unlike the other side which follows a road that is no longer used on a regular basis. You won't want to take this trail wearing sandals. The trail can get icy in the winter and will require some care to avoid slipping into Tenaya Creek.

Length: Two miles round-trip if you stop at Mirror Lake Meadow. Allow 1-2 hours. The walk to Mirror Lake gains 100 feet.

Directions to the start: This trail starts at Valley Shuttle Stop 17. If you don't want to take the shuttle you can walk from Curry Village which adds another 1.5 miles round-trip.

Facilities: There are no restrooms along the trail and you will need to bring your own water.

The Hike

Just like the Mirror Lake hike, you start from the benches and shelter at Shuttle Stop 17. You follow either the road or the unpaved foot trail to the right of the road. This trail rejoins the road at Tenaya Bridge over Tenaya Creek. A sign to the right of the bridge shows 1 mile to Mirror Lake. I have seen many unprepared people take this trail thinking it is the "normal" way to Mirror Lake. I then frequently see them turn back as the trail narrows and gets tougher. This is a way to the backside of the lake and continue as the trail closely follows the creek. After one mile the view on the left is first the lower pool of Mirror Lake and then of a large rock in the creek. This rock marks the start of Mirror Meadow. Continue on for about 100 yards and then you can go off the trail into the meadow and cross over to the creek. Your view here is of Washington Column. I like to picnic beside the creek and watch all the people on the other side wonder how I got to my side. The trail continues on what used to be a loop to the other side but has been cut by the 2009 rockslide. You can continue for another ¼ mile till you reach the rockslide but there is little more to see. After my break in Mirror Meadow I return the way I came to Shuttle Stop 17.

AHWAHNEE HOTEL TO MIRROR LAKE LOOP

This hike is one that most people don't know exists because it starts in the Ahwahnee Hotel parking lot. You can make it an out and back hike or a loop as I describe here. In the spring and after heavy rains you see Royal Arch Cascade on the way to Mirror Lake. You can shorten the distance by stopping and finishing the loop before reaching Mirror Lake. This trail ends up at the usual side of Mirror Lake as described in the Mirror Lake hike. I prefer this longer route to the usual one since it is less crowded.

When to go: Every day. This hike ends at one of the most popular locations in Yosemite so I strongly urge you to get here early, preferably before 9 am. You could also go late in the afternoon to avoid crowds, say after 5 pm in the summer. The early or late recommendation is especially important in the late spring to early fall time frame because the return part of the loop follows a bike path that gets very crowded when bikes are being rented in the Valley.

Length: Three mile loop if you go to the Upper Pool of the lake. Allow 1-2 hours. The walk to Mirror Lake gains 100 feet. Stopping your loop at Backpackers Camp and returning to the Ahwahnee is a 1 mile loop.

Directions to the start: This trail starts at the Ahwahnee Hotel at Shuttle Stop 3. From the Shuttle Stop walk toward the hotel entrance and continue past it to another group of parking lots. The trailhead starts at the far upper right corner of this public parking lot. The doormen at the hotel will direct you if you have difficulty finding the trail. Parking is extremely hard here so plan on taking the Shuttle unless you are staying at the Ahwahnee.

Facilities: There are two pit restrooms along the trail. You pass the first two times; both on the trail to the lake and again as you follow the bike path back to the Ahwahnee. The second, more crowded restroom is at the Lower Pool of Mirror Lake. You will need to bring your own water.

The Hike

From the parking lot you follow a trail all the way to the Upper Pool of Mirror Lake. If you are hiking in spring or early summer you will cross the runoff from Royal Arch Cascade in about 100 yards. This is a stream of water that I am always amazed can make so much noise as it runs down 1,250 feet over more or less unbroken granite. After another quarter mile you see a path and a sign leading to the Backpackers Camp, a camping location for those who have a wilderness permit. You can go toward the camp till you reach a bike path and turn right to return to the Ahwahnee for a relatively flat one mile loop. I prefer to continue on all the way to Mirror Lake. After another quarter mile and right before a group of rocks you can see a restroom to the right. You will go by this restroom again on the loop back.

At this point the trail goes up through a group of rocks and continues to wind through big rocks until it starts downhill just before you arrive at Upper Mirror Lake. You arrive just past Mirror Lake and turn right over a small wooden bridge to come to the lake. This is a good, but crowded area to find a rock and enjoy a snack.

To complete the loop you will continue past the upper and lower pools and follow the road along Tenaya Creek for half a mile. When you see the restroom again you will veer off the road and follow the bike path to the right, away from the creek. Another half mile takes you past the Backpacker Camp and to the Sugarpine Bridge over the Merced River. A trail on the right just before the bridge follows the river back to the Ahwahnee. I prefer to continue on the bike path, which is really a wide road, until it reaches the Ahwahnee Bridge. This bridge provides a wonderful view of the Royal Arch Cascade in season. Just after the bridge, turn right toward the hotel and walk across the hotel grounds. This provides a nice view of the more picturesque side of the Ahwahnee. Be sure to turn around and enjoy the views of Glacier Point and Half Dome from the hotel grounds. If you walk to the left of the hotel you will enjoy a view of Upper Yosemite Fall. Proceed through the hotel lobby. You may want to visit the Gift Shop or bar while you are here. Walk out the front door and turn left to return to Shuttle Stop 3.

YOSEMITE VILLAGE MEANDER

Yosemite Village is where you find the Valley Visitor Center, a museum and other facilities. This is where many visitors start their tour of the valley.

When to go: Every day. The Visitor Center hours vary by day and season but generally are open 9 am to 5 pm. You cannot drive to the Visitor Center.

Length: One mile round-trip if you walk from the Day Use Parking Lot. The walk is level.

Directions to the start: From Southside Drive turn left at Sentinel Bridge then right when you reach Northside Drive. You will turn right into the parking lot. From here I prefer to walk but you can catch the Valley Shuttle year round to Stop 2 or in the summer the Express Shuttle will drop you in front of the Valley Visitor Center at Stop P2.

Facilities: Everything you need is here.

The Meander

Starting from your car, you will walk back to the lot entrance. There you will find a yurt. (Looks like a circular tent). This is an information station staffed by volunteers from the Yosemite Conservancy. They can answer most any question you might ask. They generally staff the yurt from May 1 to the end of September. From the yurt you need to walk a short distance to Shuttle stop 1. Here you can catch a Shuttle for the quick ride to the Village or do as I do and walk there. If you catch the regular year-round Shuttle you should get off at the next Stop (#2) or you will take a side trip to the Ahwahnee Hotel which adds about 10 minutes to the trip. If catching the Express Shuttle in the summer you will only have one stop in front of the Visitor Center.

This is a walk so continue across Northside Drive and turn left immediately to cross Tecoya Road. You will follow the bike path around the DNC offices. The next building on your right is the Yosemite Art & Education Center. There is an ATM here. The Art Center offers art classes in season, normally April into October. They ask for a $5 donation per day. Classes are offered Tuesday – Friday and run for 4 hours from

10 am to 2 pm. Children under 12 must be accompanied by an adult. The center also sells all types of art supplies.

The next building contains the Sport Shop, Village Grill and Village Store. This is the place to get your best selection of supplies, food and souvenirs. Stops 2 and 10 of the Shuttle are here. Continue across Ahwahnee Drive to the Degnan's complex. Here you will find Degnan's Deli, Degnan's Loft and the Habitat Yosemite Store. I feel these two eateries are the best, reasonably priced places in the Valley (see more comments in the Where to Eat section).

The next building is the Post Office. I frequently stop in here just to drop a note to a friend. To me it's the ultimate in "wish you were here" postcard to have that Yosemite postmark on the card or letter.

The Wilderness Center is next and is where you can get backcountry camping permits and rent bear canisters. They also sell a few interesting t-shirts here. In the winter you need to go to the Visitor Center for these permits.

Next is the Ansel Adams Gallery. They are normally open from 9am to 5pm. You have likely seen some of the black and white landscape photos taken by Ansel Adams. This gallery started in 1902 as a painter's studio. Ansel married into the family that ran that studio. The name has changed and the studio now focuses on photography. His grandson is now the president of the gallery. The gallery is rather small and filled to the brim with photographs, books and posters. Photographers can still get quality film and supplies here as well. Newer photographer's work is also featured and there is normally a show of one of these artists. I always stop in here for inspiration for my poor attempts at taking pictures. In the summer the gallery offers a Photography Walk for 15 people, so reservations are critical. These start at the gallery at 9am Tuesdays, Thursdays, Saturdays and Sundays. Also at 9am Mondays from the Ahwahnee Hotel.

Next you will walk to the Valley Visitor Center. Many visitors are surprised at how hard this place is to find. At last you have arrived! Normal hours are 9am to 5pm. Inside you find helpful Park Rangers ready to advise you on how to enjoy your time in Yosemite. The relief map at the entrance helps you understand the elevation changes in the park. The exhibit halls explain the geology of the park and how wildlife adapts to survive. Be sure to make time to see the 30 minute film Spirit of Yosemite. It's especially good to see in the summer when some of the waterfalls may not be flowing. The first few minutes of the film really show you what you are missing! The bookstore here is operated by the Yosemite Conservancy and has the largest selection in the park.

Next to the Visitor Center is the Yosemite Museum. Normal hours are 9am to 5pm.This museum focuses on the cultural history of the Miwok and Paiute Indians. Basket making demonstrations are common in the summer months. A small store offers books, arts, crafts and Jewelry. Behind the museum is the reconstructed Indian Village of Ahwahnee. This was always a favorite of my son. The village features bark houses, acorn granaries and a ceremonial roundhouse.

I don't usually stop at the Yosemite Cemetery next to the museum. Some people find it fascinating to see the old grave stones. You can get a guide to the cemetery at the Visitor Center.

Retrace your steps to return to the car. The Express Shuttle will take you from Stop P2 in front of the Visitor Center. Cross the street to Shuttle Stop 9 to head back toward the parking lot on the other Shuttle. Know that you will have to ride all the way around the east end of the park through 13 stops before you reach Stop 1 and the parking lot. I always just walk back.

You can also continue walking west and will reach the start of my Lower Yosemite Fall Walk in a little under ½ mile.

LOWER YOSEMITE FALL WALK

The walk to the base of Lower Yosemite Fall is another of the extremely popular walks in Yosemite. This site can feel magical when you aren't sharing it with hundreds of new found friends so I really recommend you plan an early or late day visit here. You will also pass where John Muir built and lived in a cabin for two years. If this place was good enough for the founder of the Sierra Club it's good enough for me.

When to go: Any day there is water in the fall. Since the watershed that feeds the fall has mainly shallow, rocky, less water absorbent soil, it will dry up after the snowmelt has finished, usually in July. When this occurs there is little reason to take this walk. The Fall will flow again after a rain and late in the autumn when snow falls in the higher elevations.

Length: 1.1 miles loop. There is a slight gain in elevation of 40 feet total with the majority of the gain just before the viewing area but is otherwise a level walk. Allow about 30 minutes for the walk plus time to just look.

Directions to the start: This walk starts at Valley Shuttle Stop 6. If you don't want to take the Shuttle you can walk from the Valley Visitor Center which adds another one mile round-trip. There was parking at the start of the walk until it was replaced with a meadow in 2005. You can find limited parking along Northside Drive from the Village, but only if you are early or late in the day. Some people try to park at Yosemite Lodge at the Falls but these lots are reserved for guests of the Lodge.

Facilities: There are some of the nicest public restrooms in the park, about 100 yards from the Shuttle stop. Water is available at these restrooms. Some people will cross Northside Drive to walk to the Lodge where you can find food service.

The Walk

From Shuttle Stop 6 the walk with the best views of the Falls are to the left. The loop will bring you back to this starting point. If you go right you will initially have a view of both Upper and Lower Yosemite Falls but will soon enter trees that end the view. You walk along a bike path and across a bridge over Yosemite Creek which is the runoff from the Falls. You soon will reach the restroom facilities. I feel the best picture spot for the Lower Fall is on the opposite side of the restrooms where you find a group of picnic tables. My favorite shot is from the far left table closet to the bike path. This spot allows you to frame the Lower Fall with the pine trees along the path to the Fall.

Now continue up the wide asphalt path toward the Fall. Getting a picture along this path can be tough with all the people walking it. There are several exhibits along the path discussing the Falls. Continue up the path until you reach an open viewing area and a bridge. If you are lucky to be here in late spring or early summer the Lower Fall is roaring its full 320 foot drop. (The Statue of Liberty is 306 feet tall). The wind from the drop is quite amazing when you cross the bridge. You will get wet on the bridge when the fall is going full tilt. At this point most people just turn around and go back the way they came but you know better! You just continue forward on the loop and most of the people magically disappear. Now you have a pleasant walk through trees and fewer people. The path comes right up to the Valley wall at one point. If you look about 40 feet up the wall you see a small tree growing out of the nearly sheer cliff. Farther down, the path has a Y where you should veer right. You will see a few employee housing facilities on the left. Just before you cross the second bridge over the runoff you see a sign that simply says "Falls View" with an arrow to the right. Turn right and cross a short bridge and you will reach a small clearing along the stream. On the left is the Galen Clark Memorial Bench. On the right is a wonderful view of both the Upper and Lower Falls. Beside the creek is a small monument to John Muir. This is the site where Muir built and lived in a cabin for two years. Not bad real estate for a simple cabin.

Retrace your steps to the main path. At the junction turn right over another bridge and continue till you reach another junction. The path right will return you to the restrooms while bearing left takes you back to the shuttle stop. In going left you will soon exit the trees and if you turn back to face the Falls you will have another nice view of them. The Shuttle Stop is a few yards on the right.

SIGHTS AND ACTIVITIES I DON'T RECOMMEND

All National Parks have things that just aren't worth your time to visit. Here are my feelings about what I believe you can skip in Yosemite Valley.

Yosemite Cemetery

This cemetery contains graves of some of Yosemite's early settlers. Not my thing.

LeConte Memorial Lodge

This building commemorates a Berkeley professor who was an early activist for Yosemite and the Sierra Club. Ansel

Adams managed it for a few years in his early Yosemite days. Now it contains a library and occasionally hosts speakers. If you see a topic listed in the Yosemite Guide that interests you go ahead and visit, otherwise your time is better spent outside enjoying the Valley itself.

Four Mile Trail

This trail climbs over 3,000 feet in 4.8 miles one way up to Glacier Point. (The trail was originally 4 miles, thus the name, but was lengthened to make it easier). I say drive up to Glacier Point. The view is the same whether you drive up, take a tour bus or hike up. (Some people like to buy a one-way ticket and take the bus up and hike down). I feel this is a brutal trail, so why hurt yourself?

Upper Yosemite Fall Trail

This is another trail that goes up fast! It climbs 2,700 feet and is 7.2 miles round-trip. There are some nice views on this trail but it's really just too hard for most of us. Take the hike I call Four Waterfalls if you want a hard hike and at least see some waterfalls you can't see from elsewhere in the Valley.

Half Dome Hike

This hike is probably the most dreamed of conquest in California. Half Dome is annually conquered by thousands of people, making the trail extremely crowded at times. The route became so crowded that now the NPS requires a permit to "climb the cables" and limits these permits to 400 people per day. This trail is extremely hard covering 14 to over 16 miles, depending on the route chosen, and ascending nearly 4,800 feet, including the last 425 almost vertical feet climbing between the steel cables originally strung by the Sierra Club in 1910. This trail can be dangerous with people slipping to their death or being killed by lightening.

I climbed it as a young man and still can't believe I made it up and back down the cables. No wonder I'm nervous around heights.

What's my biggest reason for not recommending the Half Dome Hike? You can't see one of the best Valley sights from the top -Half Dome itself.

If you feel you must climb Half Dome, be sure to take the time to prepare yourself appropriately. I recommend you read and follow the advice in "One Best Hike: Yosemite's Half Dome" by Rick Deutsch, which you can order through my website.

THE PARK BEYOND THE VALLEY

This book focuses on the Yosemite Valley because that's the reason the majority of people come to Yosemite National Park. There is a lot more to the park than the Valley but I really believe you can find most of what the rest of the park offers elsewhere without hoards of people. In my opinion there are two places you should see in Yosemite outside the Valley if you have time and are visiting during the warmer months. You can't normally drive to either of these locations November to April during an average winter because the roads are closed.

GLACIER POINT

Glacier Point looms 3,242 feet above Curry Village. It's 30 miles from the Valley Visitor Center and you can drive there in about an hour. The view from here and Washburn Point just before are spectacular and shouldn't be missed if you have the opportunity. If you are coming from the south you will pass by the turnoff to Glacier Point at Chinquapin so can easily add the drive to the beginning or end of your itinerary. If you are not driving from the south you should consider adding a day to your itinerary to visit here and my next suggestion.

The Glacier Point road climbs for 16 miles from Highway 41 at Chinquapin. The road passes Badger Pass Ski area at mile 5, though you will probably miss it as no facilities are open in warm weather and it lies down a side road on the right. Just before you have driven 13 miles you will reach a small parking lot on the left where there are hiking opportunities for Taft Point or Sentinel Dome. Descriptions of these hikes are available on my website.

The road starts descending through a series of switchbacks at 14 miles and at 15 miles you reach the parking lot for the views at Washburn Point. This is a frequently skipped stopping point about a mile before Glacier Point. Some people actually mistake it for Glacier Point. I feel Washburn Point has better views of the Merced River canyon with the Giant Staircase of Nevada and Vernal Falls. These views are best from the far right of the viewing area down the short steps below the parking lot. From the far right you can also see the top of Illilouette Fall. The far left side of the viewing area provides the best view of Half Dome which looks quite narrow from this silhouette view. The face of Half Dome is not visible from this angle. There are no facilities at Washburn Point.

Continue another mile down the switchbacks and you reach the Glacier Point parking lot. I don't waste time slowly cruising the one-way beginning of the parking lot hoping for a spot. Instead I go to the end of the loop and start back uphill on the top half of the lot and find a spot almost back at the start of the lot. If I miss out on a spot here I simply go around the loop again. Incidentally there is a nice restroom at the beginning of the parking lot that frequently has lines. There are 3 more restrooms (albeit pit type so not as nice) scattered along the parking lot edges that usually have no lines.

From the parking lot it is about a 300 yard walk to the Glacier Point main view point. Along the way on the right is an amphitheater that I actually feel has better views of Half Dome than Glacier Point itself. This is where park rangers give evening talks if you are here that late. Just after this on the left is a small snack stand. Continuing up the path will take you moderately uphill toward either the Geology Hut on the right or Glacier Point straight ahead. Geology Hut has nice views of Half Dome and exhibits describing the surrounding view. The left path is designed for wheelchair access and takes you down a few short switchbacks and then back up a few switchbacks to Glacier Point. Be prepared to be awed when you reach Glacier Point and finally look down into the Valley. Everything looks miniaturized when you look down over 3,000 feet. This is another place in Yosemite where I find binoculars very useful. Be sure to look at the views from both levels of the Glacier Point area before you return to your car.

I like to be at Glacier Point as the sun sets for wonderful views of Half Dome changing colors in the alpenglow. Then after dark you get either a great star show or moonshine illuminating the surrounding countryside. Rangers will point out the constellations several nights a week. Know that, if you stay here after dark, the snack bar closes and you will need to feed yourself.

There are three ways to get to Glacier Point; you can drive, which is how most people arrive, you can take a DNC tour here or you can walk up those over 3,000 feet from the Valley. I don't recommend the hike up because it almost cost me my marriage many years ago. My recently married wife and I decided to go up to Glacier Point via the John Muir and Panorama trails. Over 8 miles and over 3,000 feet of ascent and over 8 hours later we reached Glacier Point just before our ride back to the Valley was going to give up on us. Her blistered feet made me feel so guilty that we splurged that night on a dinner at the Ahwahnee that we couldn't really afford at the time. (The real secret here: don't take a long, hard hike in new boots!)

MARIPOSA GROVE

The other place in Yosemite that you should make an effort to visit is the giant sequoia trees at the Mariposa Grove. If you have never seen a giant sequoia tree you owe it to yourself to get to the Mariposa Grove. Photos do not do these giants justice. You just can't capture the majesty of these largest living things known to man. There are two other giant sequoia groves off of Highway 120 in Yosemite, but both require at least a one mile one-way downhill hike. And those groves are much smaller than the Mariposa Grove. The Mariposa Grove is just 2 miles east of the south park entrance or 37 miles and about 75 minutes driving time from the Valley Visitor Center. Again this is convenient if you are approaching or leaving Yosemite via Fresno but much less convenient if you arrive or leave from another direction. The parking lot fills early in the summer and you may be required to take a shuttle bus from the Wawona Store 6 miles away. To avoid the shuttle bus I recommend arriving at the grove no later than 8:45 am or after 6 pm. Both times will significantly reduce the parking congestion and crowds but know that the small snack and gift shop at the parking lot will be closed.

You can see giant sequoia trees in the parking lot at the Mariposa Grove but you should either hike into the grove or take the tram tour. At a minimum I suggest you take the 1.6 mile round-trip, 400 feet elevation gain hike to the Grizzly Giant and California Tunnel Trees. There is a 50 cent brochure and map available at the trailhead (or you can print it in advance at home using the link at my website) that I recommend. It shows the trails in the Lower and Upper Groves.

My favorite way to enjoy the Mariposa Grove is to take the first tram tour on a weekday morning, usually around 9 am. The tram goes through the Lower Grove and up to the Mariposa Grove Museum. You have the option to get off the tram there. After the tram leaves you will typically be alone or close to alone in the Upper Grove. Being able to walk among the giant trees, with only the sounds of birds around you, is a truly amazing experience I whole heartedly recommend. You can walk the paths as long as you wish. If space is available, you can catch another tram back to the parking lot or if you prefer, walk the 2 miles downhill to your car.

WHAT TO DO WITH KIDS

We brought our young children to the Valley for years until they grew up and went to college. We usually just went on short hikes and they were happy as long as we had plenty of food and beverages with us. Below are the activities we found that entertained them and kept us sane.

BOOT LOT WALK

This simple walk through the Valley floor entertained our children for years. We started this tradition when our son was 5 and oldest daughter 10. The walk has enough variety to entertain the children and adults as well. There are several places to stop for restrooms and for food as well. Probably the most appreciated aspect was not one but two opportunities to play "Poohsticks". We started taking the kids to the Valley just about the time they started liking Winnie the Pooh videos. One video "A Day for Eeyore" featured the characters throwing sticks off one side of a bridge and racing to the other side to see which stick passed under the bridge first. The footbridges at Swinging Bridge and Superintendent's Bridge are perfect for this activity that can provide at least a few minutes of entertainment for children.

Since this walk is along a bike path we also found another easy way to keep the kids happy was to pack their "razor" type scooters. They could scoot along while we walked beside them (and occasionally convinced them to share). They were able to burn more energy but still complete the walk. Just be sure to keep eyes out for bikers.

SWIMMING

All kids appreciate swimming and the Merced River in the summer provides an excellent way to enjoy water. Just bring along a few sand toys for the kids, folding chairs for you and lots of towels and you can pass a few hours of play time. Be sure to pick a safe spot and position yourself downstream from the kids in case you have to perform a water rescue. Also know that this is best in July and August when the river flow is lower. It will still be cold since all this water comes from melting snow! We found the Southside drive picnic areas; Cathedral Beach, Sentinel Beach and Swinging Bridge, to be the best areas for swimming. If you are camping you can also just walk to the river and swim.

If a cold river isn't your idea of swimming fun you can swim at either Curry Village or Yosemite Lodge at the Falls. Both are free if you are staying at any of the Valley lodging options but also available for a fee to anyone who walks up. The Ahwahnee Hotel also has a pool but it is only open to guests of the hotel.

RANGER AND DNC PROGRAMS

There are daily programs geared for families with children. These are listed in the Yosemite Guide. The activities suitable for children are highlighted. Our favorites were always evening campfire programs which are available in the summer at the campgrounds and at Curry Village and Yosemite Lodge. Other activities are available all day and year round. The younger set seems to appreciate Curry Kids at Curry Village.

JUNIOR RANGERS AND LITTLE CUBS

The Junior Ranger program is a National Park program to encourage kids to get outside in the park and observe nature. If a child age 3 and up completes a list of activities they receive a Junior Ranger Badge from a park ranger. The summer edition of the Yosemite Guide has a full page listing of the required activities. There are seven requirements which include walking a trail, picking up trash and going on a ranger led program or visiting with an Indian Cultural Demonstrator. The Yosemite Conservancy also sells a "Little Cub Handbook" for ages 3-6 or a "Junior Ranger Handbook" for ages 7-13 at the Valley Bookstore and at Happy Isles. These books are not required to earn the Junior Range Badge but have additional suggestions for child friendly activities.

HAPPY ISLES NATURE CENTER

This location is open May through September from 9:30 am to 5 pm and focuses on kid friendly exhibits that encourage children to touch and learn. Frankly my children preferred to be outside hiking but I have seen other kids enjoy the facility. It is located a short walk from Shuttle Stop 16.

WHERE TO SLEEP

The best way to take advantage of the Valley is to sleep in the Valley. And staying in the Valley frequently requires advance planning. If you want to stay in the summer, during holidays and many weekends, you will need to make reservations early, sometimes as far as a year in advance.

Options: You can camp, do something I call hybrid camping, stay in furnished tents or simple cabins, or stay in motel type rooms or a quite fancy hotel.

CAMPING

There are three campgrounds in the Valley, named North Pines, Lower Pines and Upper Pines. These locations currently have a combined total of 379 camping sites that allow a maximum of 6 people and 2 cars each. All sites are very basic with no electrical outlets or showers available. Each site has a picnic table, fire ring and a bear box for your food and toiletries. The restrooms have flush toilets and cold running water. Reservations are required from March 15th through November 30th. From May 1st to September 15th you are limited to 7 days in a Valley Campsite.

Some people have strong opinions about the best campground and sites within each campground. If I want to camp in the summer, my attitude is that I'm happy to just get a spot. See my website for a link to a website that shows a picture of every camp spot in the Valley.

Reservations are through www.recreation.gov or calling 1-877-444-6777. The website is the preferred method but I use both in hopes of obtaining a summer campsite. Reservations are available up to 5 months in advance starting on the 15th of each month at 7 am Pacific time. I login into my account in advance and start trying to get a reservation at exactly 7 am. I also call at the same time. You should set up an account on the website in advance and put in your credit card information so you are ready to pay as soon as you have a site in your shopping cart. Do enough research to know which site you would like to get. Links to maps of each campground are in the links section of my website.

Campground Reservation Planning	
Desired Arrival Date	1st Date to Make Reservations
March 15 – April 14	November 15
April 15 – May 14	December 15
May 15 – June 14	January 15
June 15 – July 14	February 15
July 15 – August 14	March 15
August 15 – September 14	April 15
September 15 – October 14	May 15
October 15 – November 14	June 15
November 15 - 30	July 15
December 1 – March 14	No Reservations

The website will show you what sites are available when you put in your dates but these will change very fast as reservations for the summer typically sell out within minutes of becoming available. More than once I thought I had a campsite but it was sold to someone else before I could pay for it.

The other camping option in the Valley is at a campground known as Camp 4. This is a walk-in site that is first-come first served. There are 35 sites here and each is filled on a per-person basis with 6 people. This means each person must have their own tent, sleeping bag etc. as your party could be split over several sites so this isn't really a family camping option. This location tends to attract backpackers and mountain climbers.

NON-CAMPING OPTIONS

The remaining options in the Valley are all managed by Delaware North Companies Parks & Resorts at Yosemite or

DNC. Reservations can be made online at their website www.yosemitepark.com/Reservations.aspx or by calling 1-801-559-4884. Reservations are available 366 days in advance. If you want a holiday or summer reservation you may need to go online or call at 8 am pacific time exactly 366 days in advance. If you want to stay over a weekend during the busy seasons you will have a better chance of reservations if you start your stay on a Monday through a Thursday as you can book seven nights in a row starting 366 days in advance. Have I emphasized 366 days enough here? If you can't plan that far out you may still be able to get reservations. You will just have to try both online and the phone line as they each have some units that can only be reserved by using that method. Also, try calling 30 days or 7 days in advance as those are times by which rooms from other reservations must be cancelled to receive a refund. If reserving within 7 days of arrival you must call to make your reservation. Finally if you still don't have a reservation, just call the reservation line every night. Persistence is how you can get into a cancelled room. I have always found the reservation employees very friendly and willing to help and offer advice on getting a reservation. Also be sure to check my Yosemite Variables webpage for details on any coupons issued by the Yosemite Conservancy.

HYBRID CAMPING

DNC manages a "semi-campground" called **Housekeeping Camp**. It is usually open from late April to early October. This location has 266 units that can each hold up to 6 people. The units are 3 walls, a concrete floor and a double canvas ceiling. The 4th wall is a canvas door that slides open and shut in a fashion similar to a shower curtain. The sleeping area has a bunk bed with stacked single mattresses and a double mattress. Cots can be added to allow sleeping for up to 6 people. The mattresses are covered with plastic and you must bring your own bedding. Housekeeping Camp will rent you sheets, pillows and blankets for an additional fee. The sleeping area also includes a mirror, one electric light and two electric outlets. The ceiling extends outside over a table with chairs, a steel table for cooking with a light and electric outlet. The "patio" area has a dirt floor. A bear box for your food is just outside the privacy fence made of wood that is around 3 sides of the eating area. Also just outside your little unit is a fire ring. There is a central shower house that provides towels and soap and a laundry facility. Restrooms are spread throughout the site and also provide an outdoor wash basin to do your dishwashing.

The camp is on the Merced River and features sandy beaches though there are no lifeguards. You can't reserve specific units but can request a riverfront unit when you arrive. There is also a small camp store for basic food supplies, firewood and ice for your cooler.

Many families come to Housekeeping Camp year after year. The camp has a nice location on the river and it is easier than having to bring all your own equipment. Access to showers is also a plus over the regular campgrounds and being able to cook your own meals is a big money saver.

Even with all the advantages, I won't stay at Housekeeping Camp unless there are no other options. I find the facility offers little that I can't get elsewhere. I have my own camping gear so I prefer to pitch my own tent and save around $100 per night. You can't completely close the 4th wall, so unlike my completely shut tent, bugs can and do get into the sleeping area. In addition, I find the plastic covers on the mattresses uncomfortable to sleep on. Having the ability to cook is a big cost savings but this is almost exactly the same as cooking in a campground except the local squirrels at Housekeeping Camp are used to being fed and can be a big nuisance. My biggest issue is that Housekeeping Camp units are back to back so each unit shares a wall with one other unit. Remember the ceilings are canvas so you can hear everything your neighbor is doing (like my snoring or your ....).

CURRY VILLAGE

This location is a mash-up of tent cabins, cabins, motel units and shopping, food service and recreation facilities. This is the place for budget non-campers. Lodging units available here are 319 tent cabins, 91 insulated and heated tent cabins called Signature tent cabins, 56 cabins with bath, 14 cabins without bath and 18 motel rooms. These all add up to 498 units here. None of the units have phones or television and only the cabins and motel units have electrical outlets. Only the cabins with bath and the motel units have daily maid service. Curry Village is open only on weekends and holidays from Thanksgiving to late March. See my Yosemite Maps website page for a map of the Curry Village area.

The tent cabins are just tents with wooden floors and doors. These tent cabins are tall enough for you to stand in and can hold from 2 to 5 people depending on size. They are furnished with cots with plastic covered mattresses, some type of dresser to hold your clothes and an electric light. Sheets, blankets and pillows are provided at the end of each cot when you check in and you make your own bed. Some extra blankets are available but if you are worried about being cold you should bring your own sleeping bag or extra blankets. Towels are provided and you walk to the closest shower or rest room. The doors have padlocks on them and you must use your key to open and lock them. Since the walls are canvas you shouldn't leave anything valuable in the tent cabin. Some of the tent cabins now have safes like those you sometimes find in hotel rooms. These are welded to metal shelves in the unit. No food, beverages or even toiletries are allowed in the tent cabins. This is because bears have hyper keen noses and will go after any-thing with a scent. Canvas walls do not stop a bear, so bear boxes are provided at each tent. You can be fined for failure to use the bear boxes. Since there are potentially thousands of people sleeping here, quiet hours are from 10pm to 6am and they are enforced. More than once I have seen groups asked to leave the facilities. The "Signature" tent cabins have elec-tric heaters and seem to have a double canvas structure with insulation in between to help hold in the heat but otherwise are the same as the other tent cabins.

A step up from the tent cabins are the cabins without a bath-room. Like the tent cabins you walk to shared bathroom and shower facilities. But unlike the tent cabins you have 4 solid walls so you can keep food in the cabin though there are no cooking facilities or a refrigerator. These cabins and the cabins with a bathroom have a desk or dresser, electric heat, lights and outlets. The cabins with a bathroom also have outdoor decks or patios with chairs to help you enjoy the views. All these cabins house from 2-4 people.

Finally there are the motel units that are all located in the Stoneman House. These are simple motel type rooms that include private baths and also hold 2-4 people.

Curry Village features an array of services and recreation opportunities. There is a swimming pool free for guests in the summer and an ice rink available for a fee in the winter. There are evening programs in the summer and a bike rental shop where you can also rent a raft to float down the Merced River. Depending on the season there are food service choices including the Coffee and Ice Cream Corner, the Taqueria, the Pizza Deck and Curry Bar and the Dining Pavilion. See the Where to Eat section for more details. There is a guest lounge, especially useful in winter months, with a fireplace and tables. Puzzles and games are available at the registration desk but I recommend you bring your own. Finally there is a gift and grocery shop and the Mountain shop for outdoor gear and the Mountaineering School offices.

The location of Curry Village offers several advantages. It is the closet full service lodging facility to the hikes to Mirror Lake and my Four Waterfalls hike. It is also close to the Happy Isles Nature Center and has great views of Half Dome. A great photo opportunity is to simply go to the parking lots and look up to see Half Dome and Glacier Point above. A major advantage in the summer is parking. The lots closet to the tent cabins are reserved for Curry Village guests. Most guests don't realize there is another lot to the right of the front office. Most of the cabins are located here but any guest can park there. If nothing else is available the lot known as the Apple Tree Orchard, which is available for anyone, can also be utilized.

Curry Village accommodations are my choice of where to stay in Yosemite if I'm not camping. There are several disadvantages that keep some people from enjoying a stay here. The biggest of course is that staying here is still kind of roughing it. Sleeping in a tent is always going to be sleeping in a tent, walking down a path in the dark to find a bathroom can be scary, and entertaining the kids without a TV is also scary for some families. With all the people here it can be rather noisy and the tent cabins are close together so I recommend earplugs if you don't care to listen to your neighbors. You also may have a long walk from your car or the bus stop to your unit. For me the advantages outweigh the negatives. After all, this is a National Park and sleeping in a tent just adds to the experience for me. This is the cheapest lodging in the Valley except for camping and is usually the easiest to reserve. But the thing I really like here is the other guests. There is a shared camaraderie of being here together. And this is the most international spot in the park as you hear a multitude of languages spoken here. Most people also eat here and the deck in the summer can be a magical place to be outdoors and share stories with new friends. In the winter the guest lounge or unused portions of the Dining Pavilion provide the same feeling of camaraderie.

YOSEMITE LODGE AT THE FALLS

This is the Valley location for those who don't want to rough it in a tent or cabin. This location offers 249 motel type rooms. They all have television, telephones and small refrigerators. None of the rooms have air conditioning. The more expensive Lodge rooms are larger, feature king or double beds and have either a balcony or patio. The 19 Standard rooms are slightly smaller and are furnished with either queen or single beds. There are four family rooms that are larger and have a king bed, two single beds and a rollout couch. These rooms also have a DVD player. The rooms are spread out over 14 buildings. A few have views of Yosemite Falls and others have views of the Merced River. You cannot pre-reserve a specific room or view so ask when you check-in and hope. Parking is available through-out the facility but you can have a fairly long walk to your room. Luggage assistance is available if you need it.

This location has a gift and grocery shop, the Nature Shop, a branch post office, evening interpretive programs at the outdoor theater, a food court, the Mountain Room Lounge, the Mountain Room Restaurant, and a seasonal swimming pool, cone stand and bicycle rentals. All of the tours offered by DNC start here. Finally as the awkwardly long name suggests, Yosemite Falls is just across North Side Drive from the motel. You can see the Falls from many parts of the Lodge and even hear it when the Falls are running high.

Yosemite Lodge is not fancy. The rooms are like any chain motel room. The advantage here of course is location, location,

location. You are staying in the Valley, within easy walking distance of the 5th highest waterfall in the world. I love to stay here, wake up at sunrise, and walk over to the Falls and just sit. I am almost always alone to enjoy the view.

THE AHWAHNEE HOTEL

This is the ritziest place in Yosemite Valley. The hotel has 99 rooms in the original building and 24 cottage rooms in cabin type buildings adjoining the original building. You will want to reserve at least a "Classic Room" to ensure a good view of Half Dome, Glacier Point or Yosemite Falls. All rooms have large flat screen televisions, refrigerator, safe, bathrobes and cd player/ alarm clock. The cottages are not air conditioned. There is a year round outdoor pool. The hotel offers complimentary valet parking for guests and serves tea and cookies in the Great Lounge each afternoon. Complimentary coffee is served on the Mezzanine each morning. The hotel was retrofitted to update fire and safety systems and freshen up rooms in March of 2011. There is a bar, dining room, gift shop and sweet shop on the premises.

This is a four star hotel with phenomenal public spaces and ok guest rooms. Prices are sky high. Basic rooms start at $500 in the summer. Some find the rooms on the small side and I agree the bathrooms are a bit tiny with no real counter space available. But they do provide a small yellow rubber ducky in every bathroom and the views can be spectacular!

If you want luxury in Yosemite Valley this is the place. But many find the prices out of reach and perhaps out of line for what you get. I enjoy staying here but don't do so often because of the price and because when I pay that price I feel I have to really "stay" there and tend to not get out and enjoy the Valley. The rooms are fine but smaller. The service is nice and sitting by the big fireplaces in the Great Lounge is a treat. However those fireplaces are in public spaces so just like every place else in the Valley you have to come early or stay late to get a spot on that couch by the fire.

If you stay at the Ahwahnee try not to stay on the 1st floor. (They use the European numbering system so this is really the second floor. There are no guest rooms on the ground floor.) The hall for these rooms opens onto the Mezzanine and this in turn opens onto the Great Lounge. A nice view down into the Great Lounge from here but the openness also creates a draft that can funnel smoke from the fireplaces into the Mezzanine and down the hall. When I stayed on this level I smelled smoke every time I opened my room door.

I like the Ahwahnee and like to stay here but really can't justify the price very often. The best prices are mid-week in the winter. Since it is dark earlier in the winter I can justify staying inside more and enjoying what I am paying for. In the summer the prices are just too high and I want to be outside anyhow, so I won't stay at the Ahwahnee then.

So there are all of the sleeping options in the Valley. It really, really helps to stay in the Valley and avoid wasting time driving to and from the Valley every day. I've listed sleeping options outside the Valley at my website to help you if you just can't find a place in the Valley.

WHERE TO EAT

Yosemite Valley has a number of dining options to feed overnight guests, day trippers and park employees. This discussion covers the Valley from east to west. At the end I'll summarize your options by time of day and season and offer my suggestions on how to best feed yourself in the Valley. Note that prices for all food options are about 25 to 40% higher than comparable food prices in your home neighborhood. Remember, all that food is trucked in on the same mountain roads you traveled to get to the Valley. Visit my Yosemite Variables web page for current hours.

HAPPY ISLES

Starting from the east Valley the first option is located at Shuttle Stop 16, the stop for Happy Isles. Here you find a seasonal trailer housing a small snack bar serving cold beverages, ice cream, snacks and pre-made sandwiches. You order at a window and stand to eat as there is no seating here. This location is open only in the summer, about mid-May to mid-September and it closes around 5 pm. This is not a place to fill your belly for the day but rather a topping off location if your tummy is grumbling (or your kids' tummies) and you are in the area.

CURRY VILLAGE

West of Happy Isles is Curry Village and up to 5 dining options, depending on the season. All of Curry Village closes in the winter months except holidays and weekends. This is usually from right after Thanksgiving to the end of March. Some of these options are open if Curry Village is housing overnight guests.

The main dining option at Curry Village is the **Dining Pavilion**. This is an all-you-can-eat buffet open for breakfast and dinner. It has the biggest seating area in the Valley. The food is, well, it can remind me of my days eating at a college dorm cafeteria. Obviously not the best quality and it can get crowded here. My attitude is, if I'm really hungry this is the place to go fill the belly. Going early or late can help avoid the sometimes crowded seating. Just be aware that the food stations will get picked over at the end of the service time. The plus here of course is that you can eat and eat and eat, and the large variety of food available means you can try something else if you're not happy with what you have on your tray and someone else will clear your tray when you've finished.

For the caffeine addicts, there is a **Coffee and Ice Cream Corner** open seasonally. The coffee is ok but not as good as your neighborhood coffee shop and a fair bit pricier than home. This shop to the right of the Dining Pavilion also offers pastries, cold beverages and ice cream. Normally open early morning to late evening in the summer.

To the left of the Dinning Pavilion you find a large deck. This is the **Pizza Deck**. You order pizza or salad at a counter and sit outside and look up at Glacier Point. The pizza is ok, a little pricey, but not the best pizza in the Valley. This is a pleasant dining location, but again can be quite crowded, sometimes making finding an open table a chore. I will get my pizza in the evening and go around the corner to the outdoor seating at the Taqueria where there is not as much demand for the tables because it usually closes at 5 pm. The view is not as good but it's a seat. Also on the Pizza Deck is the **Curry Bar & Grill**. This is another counter that opens onto the deck. They serve whatever drink you could want plus things like hamburgers, wings and nachos.

I've already mentioned the **Taqueria**. It's between the Mountain Shop and the Gift/Grocery store. You order at one window and pick up at the next one. Seating is outside. This is probably the only place in the Valley that I won't eat without severe arm twisting from my travel companions. It's just greasy, over-priced taco, burrito or nacho fast food to me. Open only in the summer, usually from noon to 5 pm.

AHWAHNEE HOTEL

Next up are the food options at the Ahwahnee Hotel. You have two choices here and both are pretty pricey. First up is the **Ahwahnee Bar**. In addition to traditional beverage options, this location offers a morning coffee bar and also has a limited lunch and dinner menu. The food choices are eclectic and can range from chili to hummus to smoked fish. Prices are high. I really like coming here not for the food but for the outdoor seating on sunny afternoons. Nothing in the Valley is quite like having a waiter serve you appetizers and beverages while you bask in the sun and look up at Half Dome and Glacier Point. You may need to come early before lunch time or wait till later in the afternoon to get an outdoor table. The indoor bar area is pleasant but a bit dark for my taste.

The next choice is the **Ahwahnee Dining Room**. Reservations are recommended for all meals but required for dinner. Call (209) 372-1489 for reservations or make them online at Opentable.com. Dinner has a dress code where men are asked to wear long pants and a collared shirt and the ladies should wear a dress, skirt or slacks and a blouse. Breakfast and lunch are casual. People have very different opinions about this dining option. Some love it and others aren't impressed. Most agree that the room itself is stunning. One of my friends has described it as mountain lodge meets European castle. The room has 34 foot high ceilings with chandeliers, floor to ceiling windows and white tablecloths. At night the chandeliers appear to float in reflections on the windows. The disagreements start on the views, service, food quality and value.

If you are seated at or close to a window in the far alcove you will have a marvelous view of Yosemite Falls. All others will have trees outside the dining room or the interior of the room to ogle. Service here can be spotty. I personally have never had a bad experience with the wait staff, finding all of them to be attentive, helpful and friendly. However I have friends who swear their servers were from Mars and shouldn't have been allowed near earthlings. The food choices are varied and most diners can find something of interest to them. However when our kids were young and picky eaters, it was hard to find lunch menu items they would eat. Again, I personally have never had issues with menu choices or the food quality.

All this brings me to the discussion of value. The prices here for dinner will make it difficult for you to eat for less than $50 a person before you add any beverages. This price point leads many to expect perfection. As the previous paragraph shows, this quest for perfection can be fleeting at the Ahwahnee Dining Room. My comment for you is that I enjoy dining here but do not do so frequently. First, I am in Yosemite for the outdoors not for fine dining. Second, remember everything is trucked into the Valley so what might cost $35 in your neck of the woods is $50 here. Finally, consider that no one questions the beauty of the dining room, perhaps one of the most beautiful restaurants in the USA. For me it all adds up to coming here for dinner is an occasional treat, not one for each trip I make to Yosemite. If it's a rainy day I may come here for lunch, which is held in the same beautiful room but costs far less and is normally less crowded. For those with perhaps higher standards than mine, I suggest if you choose to dine here be ready for anything and you won't be disappointed.

YOSEMITE VILLAGE

Further west from the Ahwahnee is Yosemite Village. This location focuses on serving day visitors and has one option open year round. Located at Shuttle Stop 4, **Degnan's Deli** is my choice for the best quality food in the Valley. It's a simple location serving deli sandwiches, soup and salads but it does these quite well. You pick from a list of deli sandwiches on their menu board and can add options from a selection of beverages, snacks and desserts. It's easy to put together a moveable picnic here and that's good since there are only a few tables outside the building. More tables are around the north corner of the building and they have a view of Yosemite Falls. My only issue here is that the deli really focuses on day trippers and thus closes fairly early, usually around 5pm, so this isn't really a dinner option unless you plan ahead and get sandwiches early in the day. Also know that there is frequently a line for ordering and then another line to pay.

Next door, in the same building as the deli, is **Degnan's Café**. This is a seasonal operation from April to September that is essentially a coffee bar that also has pastries and smoothies. There are just a few tables here so usually you will be outside to eat.

Upstairs in this building is **Degnan's Loft**. You go up the stairs or elevator, order at a counter and they bring your meal to your table. They offer gourmet pizzas and this is where you find the best pizza in the Valley, although it is a bit more expensive than the Pizza Deck in Curry Village. It's also a seasonal location from April to September. They serve wine and beer here in addition to the pizza, salad and appetizers. You'll find lots of tables and a nice fireplace in the seating area. My favorite tables are at the far end from the order counter where you can look out the narrow windows at the top of the wall and see Yosemite Falls. This is the only dinning location in Yosemite Village that is open in the evening.

The last foodservice option in Yosemite Village is the **Village Grill**. Also seasonal and closing around 5pm, it is located at

Shuttle Stop 2 or 10, next to the Village Store. This is basically fast food served slowly. You walk through a counter area to order and wait for your food at the end and go outside to eat on a deck that is frequently overcrowded. They offer typical fast food hamburger type food but do have veggie, salmon and chicken burgers as well. This is not an establishment that I frequent.

YOSEMITE LODGE AT THE FALLS

The last area to find dining options in the Valley is at Yosemite Lodge. This is the last developed area and is the farthest west you will find civilization in the Valley. The main mass serving option here is the **Food Court**. This location is open year round and serves all three meals daily. As the name implies, you go to different stations which offer different food choices. The choices change with the meal time but include things like pasta, burgers, pre-made salads and sandwiches, and coffee. The quality is about like any food court in any mall in America but the prices can cause sticker shock. There is a large seating area beyond the cashiers. I prefer to take my tray outside where I can usually find tables that let me see and hear Yosemite Falls.

Open from Memorial Day to Labor Day is a snack bar next to the pool called the **Cone Stand**. It serves hot dogs, sandwiches, nachos and, of course, ice cream.

The last two dining options here are both open year round. The first is the **Mountain Room Lounge**. This is the closest the Valley comes to a sports bar because they have several big screen televisions. They have a limited menu of food items but of course offer anything you could want for a beverage. There is a nice fireplace here but for me the big draw is the tables on the patio behind the lounge. These offer a great view of Yosemite Falls and the sound of the Falls is even better. The lounge opens at noon on weekends and holidays and at 4:30 pm M-F. It closes at 11 pm nightly. Be sure to get here early if there is a sporting event you absolutely must see. I tried to get into the lounge during the 2010 World Series and all the San Francisco Giant fans made it standing room only.

The last option here is the **Mountain Room Restaurant**. This is a dinner only location that features a fantastic view of Yosemite Falls. Of course you know now from reading elsewhere that Yosemite Falls is typically dry in the summer and early fall months so that time of year you have a view of a very tall cliff. It's still quite spectacular even in the summer. Be warned that tall aspen trees may block your view if you sit too far back in the room.

This is another dining location that can elicit mixed thoughts on its merits. The menu features steak, seafood and salads. The prices are lower than at the Ahwahnee and there is usually a Chef's Choice fixed price menu of salad, main dish and dessert for around $35. My experience here has been similar to my experience at the Ahwahnee Dining room. That is the food quality is acceptable but pricey, the service is attentive and the room and view are quite nice.

This is a much more casual location than the Ahwahnee and reservations are only accepted for parties of 8 or more. Call (209) 372-1281 to make these. Open only for dinner the hours usually start around 5 pm and end around 8 pm.

That's it. Here's a quick summary of your options by meal time:

Valley Eating Options by Meal Time				
	Breakfast	Lunch	Dinner	Availability
Curry Village				
Coffee Corner	X	X	X	Seasonal
Dining Pavilion	X		X	Seasonal
Pizza Deck		X	X	Seasonal
Bar & Grill		X	X	Seasonal
Taqueria		X		Seasonal
Happy Isles Snack Bar		X		Seasonal
The Ahwahnee				
Dining Room	X	X	X	Year-round
Bar	X	X	X	Year-round
Yosemite Village				
Degnan's Café	X	X		Seasonal
Degnan's Deli	X	X		Year-round
Degnan's Loft			X	Seasonal
Village Grill		X		Seasonal
Yosemite Lodge at the Falls				
Cone Stand		X		Seasonal
Food Court	X	X	X	Year-round
Mountain Room			X	Year-round
Mountain Room Lounge		X	X	Year-round

SELF-CATERING

If you read all the eating options you probably picked up on several common themes, namely high prices and iffy quality. These facts have driven me over the years to rely on myself to feed myself for many meal times in the Valley. Of course cooking for yourself is time consuming and can also be expensive if you fail to plan ahead. And if you sleep at any of the non-camping options, cooking can be very difficult. So I always bring an ice chest with me and stock it at home with items for snacks and lunch at a minimum. Lunch is a time when I am usually away from parts of the Valley that have foodservice so I put things like sandwiches, granola bars, fruit and other snacks in my pack and don't worry about where or when to eat.

I also frequently self-cater breakfast when I want to save money or want to get onto trails and visit sites ahead of the day visitors. These breakfasts will feature things like fruit, juice, cold cereal and milk, or instant breakfast. You may prefer some type of pastry or bread. If I want something warm I break out my small camp stove and heat water for instant oatmeal and tea or coffee. Resourceful Boy Scouts, who hated washing dishes, taught me years ago how to make instant oatmeal in the bag and thus avoid washing anything but a spoon.

Now if you are staying in Curry Village, the Ahwahnee, or Yosemite Lodge there aren't too many places you can cook your own breakfast. As in none. So I go to a picnic area that allows me to do as I please. The closest to these lodging options is Church Bowl picnic area between the Ahwahnee and Yosemite Village. There is also a picnic area at Lower Yosemite Fall but no convenient parking there. Neither of these areas have grills so you can't cook your hot dogs over warm coals. Any of the other Valley picnic areas do have grills but require you to go one way out on Northside Drive and then back on Southside Drive, so I won't use them unless I am driving into the Valley and then can stop at Cathedral Beach, Sentinel Beach or my favorite at Swinging Bridge Picnic Area. See the maps page at my website for a map showing all the valley picnic locations.

Unless I am camping, I typically will go for dinner somewhere in the Valley since it's nice to have warm food at night and because it's often dark early or cold outside, so this gives you a warm place to take the kids before bedtime. Plus I don't care to take the time to cook and then clean up afterward when I've finished an active day enjoying the Valley.

Should you want to self-cater but have run out of supplies, forgot something or just didn't plan ahead there are four locations in the Valley to help you out. The biggest with the longest hours and most choices is in Yosemite Village and simply called the Village Store. This is a combination gift shop and small grocery store with just about anything you could need. Just remember that prices will be somewhat higher than at your neighborhood market. There is a parking lot with a 30 minute time limit so in theory you can run in and out quickly. However, the lot is frequently full so then you have to park in the Yosemite Village Visitor Parking Lot and walk or take the Shuttle to Stop 2. If you are parked in the Visitor Parking Lot, there are frequently picnic tables on the east edge of the lot along the Merced River. These tables have a real gem of a view of Half Dome. This store opens daily at 8 am and closes at 7 pm or later, depending on the season.

Two other locations are also open year-round but offer far fewer choices and little fresh produce or meat. These are the Gift/Grocery stores at Yosemite Lodge and Curry Village. The last location, the Housekeeping Camp General Store, focuses on needs for campers and is only open when Housekeeping Camp is open, generally April to September.

As I said, I always bring an ice chest with me and any of the above locations can supply you with ice. I normally get up early and make a quick breakfast and then hit the trails carrying my own snacks and lunch. Then I clean up a bit and head for an early dinner somewhere in the Valley. I save money and time by bringing my own breakfast and lunch, and avoid the crowds by going to dinner early. If I'm hungry later in the evening, I have my own supply of snacks and beverages to tide me over till breakfast. All this requires me to unload my car every night to avoid bear issues but I find this a minor inconvenience for the time and money savings of self-catering.

SHOPPING

Some people live to shop and the Valley has a few options for you. This discussion is focused on shopping for souvenirs, gifts, apparel and books. The Where to Eat section discusses finding groceries and camping supplies. See the variables page at my website for current hours of all these locations. There is a chart at the end here that shows all your options in the Valley.

Starting at **Happy Isles Nature Center**, you will find a few books, toys and gifts focused on pleasing children. This location is open seasonally, normally May to September.

In Curry Village you can find just about anything at the **Gift/ Grocery Shop** but this location really focuses on groceries and camping supplies and has a smaller selection of other items. Next door at the **Mountain Shop** you will find items focused on outdoor activities, especially climbing, as well as a few books, souvenirs and apparel. This is where you find the popular, "I Climbed Half Dome" shirts, which you can buy even if you didn't, but then must deal with your conscience. Both shops are open year-round with far longer hours in the summer.

At the Ahwahnee Hotel there is a **Gift Shop** and a **Sweet Shop**. The Gift Shop is where to find higher end souvenirs such as the place settings used at the Ahwahnee Dining Room. You will also find Yosemite photographs and art, and Native American crafts. The Sweet Shop has fancy chocolates as well as wine and snacks. There is also a small selection of small items you forgot, like shaving cream or a comb. These shops are also open year-round.

Yosemite Village has the broadest array of shopping options. I'll start with the **Village Store** since it has the greatest selection of souvenirs, books and Yosemite clothing. These are all between the front doors and back doors, with the grocery options off to your left if you enter from the Village pedestrian mall side. Most people will shop here for souvenirs but I believe other options are better for t-shirt type souvenirs.

The **Sport Shop** is in the same building as the Village Store. Like the Mountain Shop at Curry Village, it features supplies for outdoor activities, but with a less technical focus. There are many more clothing items here for the outdoors and most aren't really souvenir type apparel. Both the Village Store and Sport Shop are open year-round.

South of these, the **Yosemite Art & Education Center** is open from April through October and offers free art workshops Tuesday – Saturday. This location only has art supplies like canvas, paints, brushes and a few books on art subjects. The hours are from 9 am – 4:30 pm, closed from noon-1 pm daily.

In the Degnan building you find the **Habitat Yosemite** store. This is a unique store because everything in it is made from something eco-friendly such as from recycled water bottles. They feature gifts, clothing and outdoor gear that all somehow relate to Yosemite.

The next building is the **Yosemite Post Office** and believe it or not they have a few items of interest to a shopper. Specifically they have t-shirts with pictures of old postage stamps that depicted Yosemite. I believe these are the cheapest Yosemite t-shirts available. Next to the Post Office is a small building housing the **Wilderness Center**. This location is open spring through fall and focuses on issuing wilderness permits for backpackers. They have an assortment of books and maps about Yosemite's backcountry and seem to have a few unique t-shirts each year.

The **Ansel Adams Gallery** is next and you probably recognize the name and expect to find photos by Ansel Adams here. You are right but will also find work by many other photographers and artists. These works are found in prints, photographs, notecards and books. There is also a small craft and jewelry section. The Gallery also has a limited stock of cameras and tripods for rent. This store has been under the same family ownership since 1902. Open daily.

The **Yosemite Valley Visitor Center** is my favorite place to shop for books about Yosemite. There is a small bookstore to the left of the front entrance of the Visitor Center that is operated by the Yosemite Conservancy. The store has the most extensive collection of books, maps, and dvds in the Valley. They also have a small assortment of gifts and clothing. This is also the place I come for things like t-shirts. I like the designs here and appreciate that all profits go back to support the park. It doesn't hurt that I get a 15% discount since I contribute to the Yosemite Conservancy every year.

Next to the Visitor Center is the **Yosemite Museum** which has a small gift shop focusing on Native American crafts made in the museum as well as jewelry and books. The pine nut necklaces are my favorite.

The Yosemite Lodge at the Falls has two shopping locations, the **Nature Shop** and the **Yosemite Lodge Gift Shop**. The Gift Shop is similar in scope to the Curry Village Gift and Grocery and has selection of souvenirs as well as basic grocery supplies. The Nature Shop is focused on nature items and features an array of gifts from jewelry to home and garden accessories. Both locations are open daily.

Finally there is a small store at **Housekeeping Camp** that focuses on supplying basic groceries and camping supplies to those staying at Housekeeping Camp. This location is open whenever Housekeeping Camp has guests.

We have exhausted the Valley options for shopping. Here's a quick summary by location and what's available:

Valley Shopping Options					
	Souvenirs	Grocery	Camping Supplies	Gifts	Apparel
Curry Village Area					
Happy Isles Nature Center	X				
Gift & Grocery	X	X	X	X	X
Mountain Shop	X		X	X	X
The Ahwahnee					
Gift Shop	X			X	X
Sweet Shop	X			X	
Yosemite Village					
Village Store	X	X	X	X	X
Sport Shop	X		X	X	X
Habitat Yosemite	X			X	X
Post Office					X
Wilderness Center			X		X
Ansel Adams Gallery	X			X	
Visitor Center Bookstore	X			X	X
Yosemite Museum	X			X	
Yosemite Lodge at the Falls					
Gift Shop	X	X	X	X	X
Nature Shop	X			X	
Housekeeping Camp					
Grocery	X	X	X		

112

OTHER THINGS YOU MAY NEED TO KNOW

VALLEY SERVICES

This is a list of common services you may need while you visit.

ATM and Bank

There are no banks in the Valley but there is the Yosemite Credit Union located in the Post Office Building in Yosemite

Village. They have an ATM on the porch of the Art Center also in the Village. DNC has ATMs at the Ahwahnee Hotel, the Village Store, at Curry Village and at the Yosemite Lodge at the Falls.

Cell Phone Coverage

Typically you will only have cell phone access in the Valley around the four centers of services; Yosemite Village, Curry Village, the Ahwahnee Hotel and Yosemite Lodge at the Falls. Glacier Point also seems to get coverage. Anywhere else will depend on your phone, carrier and weather conditions. Bottom line: don't count on cell service unless you are in the Valley, close to civilization.

Internet Access

If you are staying at any of the DNC managed properties; the Ahwahnee Hotel, Yosemite Lodge at the Falls or Curry Village you will have access to Wi-Fi during your stay. Other visitors can pay for access at the Yosemite Lodge. A few internet terminals are available for a fee at Degnan's Café.

Medical and Dental

There is a Medical Clinic between Yosemite Village and the Ahwahnee Hotel. If you have an emergency you should dial 911. The clinic is available 24 hours for urgent care at 209-372-4637. If you are really critical you will be flown by helicopter to Fresno or Modesto. There is also a Dental Clinic at the same location for basic dental services 209-372-4200.

Showers and Laundry

If you are in need of a shower you can go to either Curry Village or Housekeeping Camp and pay for access. Laundry facilities are available in season at Housekeeping camp.

Pets

Pets are very restricted in the Valley and are not allowed on any trails out of the Valley. DNC operates a dog kennel from Memorial Day to Labor Day but it has strict limitations and not a lot of space 209-372-8348.

Gas

There are no public gas stations in the Valley so be sure you fill up in the last major town outside of the park. There are gas stations inside the park at Wawona, Crane Flat and Tuolumne Meadows. Note that the gas station in El Portal is notorious for being very high priced so you should fill up in Mariposa if you are coming to the Valley on Highway 140.

Road Conditions

For conditions inside the park call 209-372-0200. For condition of the roads leading to the park call CALTRANS 800-427-7623.

Lost and Found

If you think you lost it at a NPS facility or on a trail call 209-379-1001. If you left something at a restaurant, shop or hotel call DNC at 209-372-4357.

GETTING AROUND THE VALLEY ON THE SHUTTLE SYSTEM

The NPS provides a Shuttle Bus that serves the east portion of the Valley. You should plan to use this service. Parking can be hard to find, so once you have managed to park, try not to move your car until you leave the Valley.

The Shuttle has 22 stops and normally operates from 7 am to 10 pm. Shuttles are more frequent during the 9 to 5 timeframe. The Yosemite Guide has a map of the Shuttle route or you can also pick one up when you board a Shuttle. Some of the drivers can be pretty entertaining as they drive you around the Valley.

Here's a summary of what you'll find close to each Shuttle Stop:

Valley Shuttle Stop Highlights	
Stop	Highlights
1	Valley Visitor Parking Lot End of Housekeeping Camp Bridge Walk
2	Village Store Village Grill Sport Shop Yosemite Art & Education Center / ATM
3	Ahwahnee Hotel Ahwahnee Bar Ahwahnee Dining Room Sweet Shop Ahwahnee to Mirror Lake Loop Hike

4	Degnan's Deli
	Degnan's Café
	Degnan Loft
	Habitat Yosemite
	Walk to Post Office
	Walk to Wilderness Center
	Walk to Ansel Adams Gallery
5	Valley Visitor Center
	Yosemite Conservancy Bookstore
	Yosemite Theater
	Yosemite Museum
	Yosemite Village of the Ahwahnee
	Yosemite Cemetery
6	Lower Yosemite Fall Walk
	On loop of Boot Lot Walk
	Cooks Meadow across road
7	Camp 4
	Trailhead for Upper Yosemite Fall Trail
8	Yosemite Lodge at the Falls
	Mountain Room
	Mountain Room Lounge
	Food Court
	Cone Stand
	Bike rentals
	DNC Tour Departures
	Swimming Pool
	Gift Shop
	Nature Shop
9	Across from Stop 5
10	Across from Stop 2
11	Sentinel Bridge
	Cooks Meadow
	Walk ½ mile to Yosemite Chapel
	On Boot Lot Walk
	Superintendent's Bridge ¼ mile walk

12	Housekeeping Camp LeConte Memorial Lodge Housekeeping Camp General Store Public laundry and shower facilities Start of Housekeeping Camp Bridge Walk
13A	Curry Village Activities Center Raft and bike rentals Ice skating rink
13B	Curry Village Check-in Gift & Grocery Yosemite Mountain Shop Yosemite Mountaineering School Office Dining Pavilion Pizza Deck Ice Cream & Coffee Corner Taqueria Swimming Pool
14	Visitor Parking Lot Camping Reservation Center Stoneman Meadow ¼ mile walk Alternative for Stop 13B
15	Upper Pines Campground Wilderness Trailhead Parking East end of Curry Village tent cabins
16	Nature Center at Happy Isles Happy Isles Snack Bar Start of Four Waterfalls Hike
17	Mirror Lake Trailhead Mirror Lake (Meadow) Hike Backside of Mirror Lake Hike
18	Stables North Pines Campground Backpackers Overnight Camp
19	Lower Pines Campground Upper Pines Campground across road

20	Across from Stop 14
21	Across from stop 13A
1	Back to Valley Visitor Parking Lot

You may have noticed that several of the stops are across a road from one another, specifically Stops 2 and 10, 5 and 9, 13A and 21 and 14 and 20. These "cross stops" can allow you to avoid spending time looping through various parts of the east Valley. For example, if you get on the Shuttle at Stop 8 at Yosemite Lodge at the Falls and want to go to the Ahwahnee Hotel, you would have to ride all the way to Stop 21 and continue on through Stop 1 until you finally reach Stop 3 at the Ahwahnee. Instead, you could get off at Stop 10 and cross the road to Stop 2 and board the next Shuttle going to Stop 3. A BIG time savings.

OTHER SHUTTLE ROUTES

In the busy summer months there are two other Shuttle routes available. Both only run from 9 am to 6 pm so you have to be especially careful on the second route to avoid stranding yourself a long walk away from the civilized part of the Valley. The first, called the **Express Shuttle**, runs from inside the Valley Day Visitor Parking Lot (P1) directly to the Valley Visitor Center (P2 also Stop 5 on the Valley Shuttle route) and then returns directly to the parking lot. This eliminates the jaunt over to the Ahwahnee Hotel.

The second shuttle is called the **El Capitan Shuttle** and starts in front of the Valley Visitor Center and loops though a portion of the west Valley. Here are the stops on this route:

El Capitan Shuttle Stop Highlights	
Stop	Highlights
E1	Valley Visitor Center
E2	Camp 4 Trailhead for Upper Yosemite Fall Trail
E3	El Capitan Picnic Area
E4	El Capitan Bridge Walk ¼ mile to El Capitan Meadow
E5	Four Mile trailhead Walk ¼ mile to Swinging Bridge Picnic Area and Start of Boot Lot Walk
E1	Back to Valley Visitor Center Stop 5 of Valley Shuttle Stop P2 of Express Shuttle

VALLEY WILDLIFE

Many people come to the Valley in hopes of seeing native animals as opposed to the nearly 4 million human animals that visit annually. Most want to see a bear. I've got bad news for you. In over 30 years of visits I have never seen a bear in the Valley. I must admit that I have heard one EVERY night I camped in the Valley, but I have just rolled over and snuggled back to sleep in my bag because I knew I had properly stored my food and the bear was making a meal out of someone else's future breakfast. There are over 70 different kinds of mammals in the park but you are most likely to see squirrels and chipmunks raiding the food of unsuspecting visitors. You will almost never see mountain lions, bobcats or badgers. Occasionally you may glimpse a coyote if you are in a meadow early or late in the day.

The one mammal I regularly see in the meadows is mule deer. I have seen them in all the meadows and even in the visitor parking lot at Curry Village that happens to be in an old apple orchard that still bears fruit. Amazing that the deer seem to know when the apples are falling. You should be careful around deer as they have sharp hooves and antlers that can cause a lot of damage to a human. Don't ever feed any of the Valley wildlife, including the deer.

The Park has over 240 kinds of birds and these are what you are most likely to see in the Valley. Or perhaps hear them if you get away from the human animals a bit. You'll know you are around a Steller's Jay if you hear a kind of screeching sound or notice a blue colored bird hoping around your picnic table. Other common birds are the acorn woodpecker, with black and white feathers and red head, or a black-headed grosbeak, with black, white and orange colors.

The Valley also has a number of reptiles and amphibians. There are western fence lizards which are common and have a brown gray top side and a bluish underside. Frogs are common but you will probably hear and not see them around the river and especially near Happy Isles Nature Center. You may see a garter snake but not normally a rattlesnake in the Valley. The other common amphibian is the brown orange California newt, which is frequently seen after rain.

There are fish in the Merced River. The only native game species is the rainbow trout. Other trout include the brook, brown and cutthroat. The NPS service ended the practice of stocking fish in Yosemite.

BEAR RULES

The black bears of the Valley are ravenous and will eat just about anything. Years ago the park service would put out trash nightly to feed the bears and entertain the tourists. This led to bears becoming accustomed to people and the high calorie content of people food. Hey, would you rather eat grubs and acorns or leftover burgers and pizza? Bears and people for some reason have trouble mixing together and bears have to be killed every year to prevent humans being hurt. It's really our fault if a bear is killed because we can put that tempting food out of reach of a bear. Unfortunately, many people don't realize that to bears, food can include things like empty grocery bags, ice chests, canned and bottled goods and smelly things like toiletries or unwashed cooking utensils. So there are rules about what we leave where. When you check into a lodging place or campground you will receive a page that describes the food storage rules and be asked to initial that you have read it. Don't just read it, follow the rules or you can be fined and even be thrown out. And that's in addition to the big repair bill you face to remove that new zipper feature a bear added to your car. Those darn bears have amazing car openers!

You can leave food in your car in the Valley only during the day but even then must have it out of sight of a potential marauder. I always bring a few towels to cover up anything I might have in the back seat. You must empty the car of any food item at night and either put it into a bear box or a motel room. Basically you must remove anything that smells or looks like it might contain food. This means the trunk too unless you want to have a new way to get into it! Also know that crumbs or even seats that have spills on them could attract a roving bear. A recent study found that minivans were much more likely to have bear break-ins than other vehicles. Why? Probably because minivans usually mean kids and kids tend to spill and make messes, thus leaving temptation for a bear even when the vehicle is empty. When we had young children, we always vacuumed our minivan before we headed to the Valley to try and ward off this potential trouble.

VALLEY PLANTS

The Valley has hundreds of different plant types. The meadows have all types of grasses and wildflowers. The wildflowers typically bloom in the Valley meadows in May. My favorite is the easy to identify, purple colored, lupine. You will most likely see California black oak trees and ponderosa pine trees around the Valley with occasional incense cedar trees. You can also find mountain dogwood trees blooming in May in the Bridalveil Fall and Tenaya Creek areas. The Valley isn't known for having great autumn colors but you can see some colored leaves in late October to November in places like El Capitan Meadow and Cooks Meadow.

This is an obviously short list of plants, so you should read one of the books I list in my website if you want more information on the flora of the Valley.

HOW THE VALLEY WAS MADE

I had to take several science classes in college and one was geology. Unfortunately, I don't remember much of that class since I was really there because my girlfriend was also there. So this is a really simple explanation of how we got the Yosemite Valley.

Millions of years ago the Merced River flowed through a shallow valley but then the Sierra Nevada Mountains began to slowly rise and push the land upward. The river cut more deeply into the granite as the land rose and this created a v-shaped valley. Then the climate cooled and the mountains were covered by ice and glaciers. The glaciers moved through the valley and carved up the granite so that we have the u-shaped Yosemite Valley walls we see today. The melting glaciers left debris at the west end of the Valley and that dammed up the Merced River thus creating a lake that filled with sediment over thousands of years and left us with the level Valley floor we see today.

As I said, this is extremely basic so if you want more information on the geology of the Valley you should visit the Valley Visitor center or read one of the geology books I list in my website.

A Very Brief Valley Historical Timeline	
? BC	People lived in the Valley for thousands of years
1833	Fur trappers see Valley
1851	Mariposa Battalion enters Valley
1864	Yosemite Grant. Signed by Lincoln. Gives Yosemite Valley and Mariposa Grove to State of California to hold for public use. First public wilderness park in the world
1868	John Muir first visit to Valley
1874	First road into Valley
1890	Yosemite National Park established as 3rd National Park. Excludes the Valley!
1891	US Cavalry troops patrol park
1906	Yosemite Grant transferred to federal jurisdiction
1914	Park administered by civilian employees
1916	The National Park Service (NPS) established
1970	Shuttle Bus system established in the Valley
1996	Rock fall damages Happy Isles Nature Center
1997	Heavy January rains cause extensive flooding. Valley closed for 3 months. Riverside campgrounds permanently closed.

LINKS AND MAPS

My website, www.KennBennetts.com has every link promised in this book (plus many more). Why not list them here or in the text? Because you would have to type them in anyhow, they tend to change and I think they just look junky. So instead I'm sending you to a central location where it will be easy to link to any web location you want without having to worry about mistyping or changes. The Yosemite specific information on my website is at www.KennBennetts.com/Yosemite.

Ok, so where are the maps? I thought long and hard about whether I should include maps in this book. You may have noticed my conclusion was no. Why, you ask? Well one reason is because I can't draw. Another is because I didn't think it would really help you if I just copied the free National Park Service maps of Yosemite and put them on the small pages here. And lastly I decided it would just jack up the price you had to pay for this book if I paid someone else to make my version of the perfectly useful NPS maps. So again I send you to my website where you will find links to the NPS maps you need to enjoy Yosemite. That way you can print them if you want or just wait and pick them up at a park entrance or visitor center. I also have suggestions for other maps you might consider buying if you want more than the NPS offers. You will find all this at www.KennBennetts.com/Yosemite/maps.

ABOUT THE AUTHOR

Ok first thing, yes my name is Kenn and not Kenneth and my birth certificate is available to prove it. And yes it has that unusual double n that makes it so I can never get anything off those racks of mugs with names printed on them. My mother thought it looked nice when written together with Bennett.

That's nice, you say, but why are you any good at writing about Yosemite? Well because I've been there. A lot. And I believe I can help you enjoy it because I've learned to travel well. Again a lot. 49 states and 17 countries at last count (and no I won't tell you which state I haven't been to – yet). I'm kind of retired these days so thought I could put my knowledge to use and help people to better enjoy a place I've come to love in visits stretching over 30 years.

PHOTO INFORMATION

All of the photos for this book were taken by Kenn Bennett except the back cover author photo taken by Lori Bennett and Ahwahnee Bridge photo taken by Kristen Bennett. You can see these photos and more in color at www.KennBennetts.com/Yosemite/photos.

- Cover photo - Half Dome from Shuttle Stop 6

- Back over photo – Author at Valley View with Bridalveil Fall over right shoulder

- Inside cover photo – Upper Yosemite Fall from Yosemite Village

- Introduction photo – Valley View

- What to See photo – Vernal Fall from trail to Clark Point

- What to Do photo – Ahwahnee Bridge

- Hikes and Walks photo - Giant Staircase from Washburn Point

- I Don't Recommend photo – Bear Damage Warning Sign in Curry Village parking lot

- The Park Beyond the Valley photo – Giant Sequoia Trees in Mariposa Grove

- What to Do with Kids photo – Mirror Lake with reflection of Mt Watkins on left and Ahwiyah Point on left

- Where to Sleep photo – El Capitan from Northside drive

- Where to Eat photo – Dogwood blossoms along Tenaya Creek

- Shopping photo – Nevada Fall from Clark Point

- Other Things photo – Shuttle Bus with Half Dome at Shuttle Stop 6

- Did You Enjoy? photo – My trusty folding chair along Merced River at Cathedral Beach Picnic Area

DID YOU ENJOY THE YOSEMITE VALLEY?

If you have thoughts on this book, corrections I should make or want to share your own Yosemite Valley tips, please go to www.KennBennetts.com/feedback. I really do appreciate your input and may use it on the website or in future books.

COMING SOON!

Kenn Bennett's Secrets to the following National Parks:

Sequoia
Joshua Tree
Death Valley

Published by:
Negiup Publishing LLC
PO Box 7452
Thousand Oaks, CA 91359
www.NegiupPub.com

Printed in U.S.A. First Edition, May 2011.

For the latest updates visit www.KennBennetts.com

ISBN: 0983538700
ISBN-13: 9780983538707

Made in the USA
Lexington, KY
01 June 2011